SHORT CUTS

INTRODUCTIONS TO FILM STUDIES

OTHER TITLES IN THE SHORT CUTS SERIES

RELIGION AND FILM

CINEMA AND THE RE-CREATION OF THE WORLD

S. BRENT PLATE

WALLFLOWER

LONDON and NEW YORK

First published in Great Britain in 2008 by
Wallflower Press
6 Market Place, London W1W 8AF
www.wallflowerpress.co.uk

A catalogue record for this book is available from the British Library

ISBN 978-1-905674-69-5

Series design by Rob Bowden Design

Printed in the UK by Cromwell Press, Trowbridge, Wiltshire

CONTENTS

ACKNOWLEDGEMENTS

Earlier versions of chapters 3 and 4 were originally published in *Post-scripts: The Journal of Sacred Texts & Contemporary Worlds*, 1, 2–3 (2005), 259–75; and Charles Lippy (ed.) *Faith in America*, volume 3 (2006), Westport, CT: Praeger, 101–18. I would like to thank the publishers for permissions to reprint these pieces.

Like filmmaking, book writing depends on a significant production crew. In recent years, I have been fortunate to work, talk, eat, drink and commune with many great people who implicitly and explicitly have contributed to this book. Therefore, I want to thank my co-editors, co-directors and co-producers: Yoram Allon, Megan Ammann, Timothy Beal, Christopher Boesel, Linda Ehrlich, Betsy Flowers, Doug Gay, Simon Halliday, David Jasper, Tod Linafelt, Darren J. N. Middleton, David Morgan, David Nienhuis, Brittney Smith and my wonderful colleagues in Beasley Hall, TCU. Each one has helped me see differently. Finally, many thanks to my Executive Producers: Edna Melisa, Sabina Elli and Camila Elli. I dedicate this book to my late friend, Doug Adams, whose smile continues to shine in my mind's eye.

PREFACE

This book makes an argument by analogy. I argue that religion and film are *like* each other, and that their similarities exist on a formal level. As a preliminary demonstration of the relations, consider the following two quotes:

> Whatever its shape, the [camera] *frame* makes the image finite. The film image is bounded, limited. From an implicitly continuous world, the frame *selects* a slice to show us ... Characters enter the image from somewhere and go off to another area – offscreen space. (Bordwell & Thompson 2001: 216; emphasis added)

> The most salient characteristic of ritual is its function as a *frame*. It is a deliberate and artificial demarcation. In ritual, a bit of behaviour or interaction, an aspect of social life, a moment in time is *selected*, stopped, remarked upon. (Myerhoff 1977: 200; emphasis added)

Two well-known scholars of film and a well-known anthropologist discuss their respective objects of enquiry – cinematography, ritual – describing their functions with similar language. Cameras and rituals *frame* the world, *selecting* particular elements of time and space to be displayed. These framed selections are then projected onto a broad field in ways that invite viewers/adherents to become participants, to share in the experience of the re-created world. The altar and the screen are thus structured and function in comparable fashion. I will argue in the introduction that we can see these commonalities more fully if we understand the ways filmmaking and religion-making are bound under the general guise of *worldmaking*.

Films and religions arise from and play themselves out within specific cultures, yet each can be generically recognised in spite of cultural differences because each uses the same tools and raw materials. I am not blithely eliding cultural differences here, simply saying that no matter what culture a film comes from they all use cameras and projectors and come into being through procedures such as cinematography and editing. The same is true of the myths, rituals and symbols of religion: even if drastically different from setting to setting, all religions seem to include some form of them as part of their tradition. And because religion and film are structured like each other, they have a tendency to borrow from each other, unwittingly or not. This latter point will require further argument and forms one of the key theoretical emphases of this book.

That said, this is not a book that surveys the various manifestations of religion *in* film (for example, studies of 'images of Jesus/the Buddha/ angels on film', or what I call the 'spot-the-Christ-figure' method), much less is it a work of theology and film. Nor does it remain within a single genre, regional cinema or time frame, or work from any single religious perspective. Rather, by examining films and genres from around the world – including most prominently Hollywood blockbusters, Danish and Japanese fiction, avant-garde and documentary films – I aim to emphasise some of the underlying dimensions of what is called 'film form', and then relate these to the underlying forms of religious structures found around the world. Thus, I retain the more neutral and ambiguous terminology, 'religion and film', holding up both sides with more or less equal weight.

While 'religion and film' is a relatively recent and increasingly vital field of scholarly enquiry within religious studies, the relation between religion and film is as old as cinema itself. If the origin of cinema dates to the Lumière brothers' first public screening for a paying audience in December 1895, then the first decade of cinema saw at least half a dozen filmed versions of the life and passion of Jesus Christ, including those made by the inventors of film themselves, Thomas Edison and Louis Lumière. Not long after, the 'father' of Indian film, D. G. Phalke (see 2007), was inspired by a film of the life of Christ and set out to project the pantheon of Hindu deities onscreen. Film theorist André Bazin noted, 'The cinema has always been interested in God' (1997: 61), while director Jean Epstein went one step further: 'I would even go so far as to say that the cinema is polytheistic and theogonic ... If we wish to understand how an animal, a plant, or a stone can inspire fear, respect, or horror, those three most sacred sentiments, I think we must watch them on the screen, living their mysterious, silent lives, alien to the human sensibility' (2007: 52). And all of this occurred decades before there was such a phrase as religion and film.

Yet, while the actual relation between the two is now over a century old, the critical academic enterprise of religion and film is just getting its legs. Early studies, the sporadic titles appearing from the late 1960s to the 1980s, were particularly grounded in Paul Tillich's theology of culture (1964). From a humanistic point of view, film was understood to tell us about the human condition, thus attention to film helps us understand more about this thing called humanity, its destiny and purpose. The works of Pier Paolo Pasolini, Carl Theodor Dreyer, Robert Bresson, Ingmar Bergman and other European auteurs, alongside Akira Kurosawa and Yasujiro Ozu, were prominent in these studies. By the late 1980s a new wave of scholars, chiefly in religious studies, reacted to this earlier paradigm that found religion and film only in 'serious', art-house films. In contrast, this second wave of scholars began to pay attention to popular Hollywood films because, it was argued, this is what 'the masses' watch and thus when we investigate popular films we find out something about mass culture in general. Both of these earlier movements tended to emphasise the verbal narratives of the films, and thus the studies were often indistinguishable from literary interpretations.[1]

In the past decade a third wave of religion and film studies has emerged with at least two primary concerns. The first is a move away from literary models of interpretation towards medium-specific models; that is, scholars from religious studies are now engaging more fully with film criticism and theory. (Unfortunately, few film studies scholars have taken on issues of religion in any serious and critical way.) The second concern is a move from formal and narrative analyses of specific films, towards audience reception and how the viewing of film itself is similar to participation in religious ceremonies. This book situates itself within this third wave. The first part relates elements of film form, gleaned from theoretical analyses of film, to theories of religion, thinking through the ways myths and rituals might be seen by way of cinematography, editing and *mise-en-scène*.

The second part of the book is concerned with how films affect viewers in bodily and ritualistic ways, considering the analogy of religion and film from a functional standpoint.[2]

INTRODUCTION: WORLDMAKING ONSCREEN AND AT THE ALTAR

> All invention and creation consist primarily of a new relationship
> between known parts. (Deren 1987: 69)

The lights dim, the crowd goes quiet and viewers begin to leave the worries
of this world behind, anticipating instead a new and mysterious alternative world that will soon envelop their eyes and ears. The screen lights up
with previews of coming attractions, each beginning with that same deep,
male voice:

> 'In a world where passion is forbidden...'
> 'In a world where you must fight to be free...'
> 'In a world where your best friend is a dog...'

Films create worlds. They do not passively mimic or directly display what is
'out there', but actively reshape elements of the lived world and twist them
in new ways that are projected onscreen and given over to an audience.
The attraction and promise of cinema is the way films offer glimpses into
other worlds, even if only for ninety minutes at a time. We watch, hoping to
escape the world we live in, to find utopian projections for improving our
world or to heed prophetic warnings for what our world might look like if we
do not change our ways. In the theatre we live in one world while viewing
another, catching a glimpse of 'what if?'

Yet, in the practice of film viewing, these two worlds begin to collide,
leaking ideas and images across the semi-permeable boundaries between
world-on-screen and world-on-the-streets. Such world-colliding activity
is entertainingly exemplified in Woody Allen's *The Purple Rose of Cairo*

(1985). Here, the fluidity between the worlds is enacted when the actor named Tom Baxter (played by Jeff Daniels) steps down off the screen and enters the 'real world' in which Cecilia (Mia Farrow) sits, seeking relief from her otherwise troubled life. In Allen's film, two worlds cross and both characters are altered because of their shared desires that transcend the boundaries of the screen. Nonetheless, *The Purple Rose of Cairo* does not let go of the fact that there *is* a screen in place between Tom and Cecilia. The screen is a border that is crossable, yet there are distinctions between the two sides, for example when Tom enters Cecilia's world and takes her out for a night on the town and tries to pay for dinner with the fake prop money he has in his pocket. The couple eventually come to realise they live in two worlds and a permanent connection is impossible. Of course, all this takes place *on* screen, and not in the real world per se.

Woody Allen's film, while delightfully self-referential about the experience of cinema, also tells us much about the experience of religion. As I argue throughout this book, religions function like films and vice versa. Through the myths, rituals, symbols, doctrines, sacred times and places and ethical components of religions, the faithful are presented with alternate worlds, prescriptions for a better life and imaginative tools for re-viewing the world as it is. Religions provide promises, warnings and compelling narratives for behaving in particular (and often peculiar) ways. In the midst of this, communities of religious adherents work out their lives betwixt and between the two worlds. Powerful stories in the form of myths keep religious imaginations inspired, while aesthetic performances in the form of rituals keep human bodies moving to a rhythm. Even so, when the story is over, when the chanting has finished, when the feast has been eaten, we return to our everyday world. The two worlds seem to remain in a state of separation, yet there are many avenues for connection between them.

Religion and film are akin. They both function by recreating the known world and then presenting that alternative version of the world to their viewers/worshippers. Religions and films each create alternate worlds utilising the raw materials of space and time and elements, bending each of them in new ways and forcing them to fit particular standards and desires. Film does this through camera angles and movements, framing devices, lighting, costume, acting, editing and other aspects of production. Religions achieve this through setting apart particular objects and

Very Imp.

key to the book

periods of time and deeming them 'sacred', through attention to specially charged objects (symbols), through the telling of stories (myths) and by gathering people together to focus on some particular event (ritual). The result of both religion and film is a re-created world: a world of recreation, a world of fantasy, a world of ideology, a world we may long to live in or a world we wish to avoid at all costs. As an alternative world is presented at the altar and on the screen, that projected world is connected to the world of the everyday, and boundaries, to a degree, become crossable.

This book, then, is about the connection of the world 'out there', and the re-created world onscreen and at the altar, and how these worlds have a mutual impact on one another. The impact, furthermore, is often so great that participants do not see differences in the worlds but rather a seamless whole. Religious worlds are so encompassing that devotees cannot understand their personal worlds any other way; filmic worlds are so influential that personal relationships can only be seen through what has been observed onscreen. My hypothesis is that by paying attention to the ways films are constructed, we can shed light on the ways religions are constructed and vice versa. Film production borrows millennia-old aesthetic tactics from religions – at the dawn of the twentieth century film-makers were more self-conscious about this than they are at the start of the twenty-first century – but contemporary religious practices are likewise modified by the pervasive influence film has had on modern society. In general, the first part of the book will focus on similarities in aesthetic tactics between religion-making and filmmaking. The second part focuses attention on the ways religious practices, especially rituals, have incorporated the recreated worlds of film and the ways in which film viewing operates like a ritual.

Herein, I play the role of editor, or perhaps of *bricoleur*, juxtaposing film theory and religious theory in order to highlight the ways both religion and film are engaged in the practice of *worldmaking*. As intimated by avant-garde filmmaker Maya Deren in the epigraph above, invention and creation do not operate by bringing something into being 'out of nothing' (a troubling myth of creativity perpetuated by Christian theology and a romantic view of the modern artist alike), but by taking what is already known and creating a new relationship. There is nothing new under the sun, but there are new relationships between old substances. Along these lines, I adopt the language of the great Soviet filmmaker Sergei Eisenstein, who in 1929 wrote of the social value of 'intellectual montage' (see 1992b), in which new and revolutionary ideas might spring from the juxtaposition of previously separate images. And to be interdisciplinary about it, I juxtapose Eisenstein with the words of religionist Wendy Doniger who suggests of the comparative study of religion: 'The comparatist, like the surrealist, selects pieces of *objets trouvés*; the comparatist is not a painter but a collagist, indeed a bricolagist (or a *bricoleur*), just like the mythmakers themselves' (1998: 77). Worlds, religious and filmic, are made up of borrowed fragments and pasted together in ever-new ways; myths are updated and transmediated, rituals reinvented, symbols morphed. The theoretical images in this book will be familiar to many readers, as I rely on relatively standard theories of religion and film, but by lining them up side by side I hope to aid an understanding of the relation between them.

The remainder of this introduction will briefly examine the concept of worldmaking and re-creation more fully from a religious studies standpoint, before introducing the ways films participate in worldmaking activities through filmmaking techniques. After drawing up a brief outline of the chapters of this book, I chart what I hope will be a *critical religious film theory*.

I. Religious worldmaking and re-creation

In the background of my argument are the world-building and world-maintaining processes of religion brought out in Peter Berger's now-canonic work, *The Sacred Canopy* (1967). We humans, this sociologist of religion suggests, collectively create ordered worlds to provide us with a sense of stability and security, 'in the never completed enterprise of building a humanly meaningful world' (1967: 27). Reality, like religion and like cinema, is socially constructed, allowing its members to engage with it on deeply-felt, personal levels. The role of cultural products such as film offers conduits of significance between the individual and the cosmic order of the universe. And if culture staves off meaninglessness at the societal level, religion does so at a cosmic level by constructing a 'sacred canopy' that keeps the threatening forces of chaos at bay.

Ever important is the grounding of human laws and regulations in cosmic structures. The *nomos* (the meaningful societal order) must be in synch with the *cosmos* (the universal, metaphysical order). There is a dialectical, ongoing process between the human and divine realms, and it is religion that supplies the link: 'Religion implies the farthest reach of man's self-externalisation, of his infusion of reality with his own meanings. Religion implies that human order is projected into the totality of being. Put differently, religion is the audacious attempt to conceive of the entire universe as being humanly significant' (Berger 1967: 27–8).

Indeed, Berger himself states that while most of history has seen religion as key to creating such a meaningful totality, in modern times 'there have been thoroughly secular attempts at cosmisation' (1967: 27). Science has most importantly made the attempt, but here I am suggesting that we think about cinema as another audacious attempt. Cinema may be part of the symbol-creating apparatus of culture, yet it can also aspire to more, to world-encompassing visions of the nomos and cosmos.

The philosopher Nelson Goodman similarly understands the culturally/socially constructed nature of the world, particularly as demonstrated in his book, *Ways of Worldmaking* (1978). Approaching the topic from an epistemological standpoint rather than Berger's sociological one, Goodman draws an analogy between philosophy and the arts to understand how we humans go about creating worlds around us. Goodman suggests, 'Much but by no means all worldmaking consists of taking apart and putting together, often conjointly: on the one hand, of dividing wholes into parts and partitioning kinds into subspecies, analysing complexes into component features, drawing distinctions; on the other hand, of composing wholes and kinds out of parts and members and subclasses, combining features into complexes and making connections' (1978: 7). The activity of world creation is a process of taking things apart and putting them back together, of reassembling the raw materials available, of dissection and analysis and of mending fragments. Such philosophical/religious activity is easily translatable in terms of filmmaking, through the framing of space via cinematography and reprojecting it onscreen, or with its partitioning of time through edited cuts and then the recombining done in the editing room.

I borrow the language of worldmaking from Berger and Goodman, but in the background is the work of Immanuel Kant, Émile Durkheim and others. Meanwhile, the scholar of comparative religion, William Paden, has synthesised many of these studies, offering evocative and accessible ways to approach both religion and film. In Paden's view religions each posit and construct their own version of 'the' world through various organising categories made up of the activities, behaviours, beliefs, language and symbol usages of persons and communities. By looking at religious systems as 'worlds', as opposed to the relatively disembodied examination of texts and doctrines, the student of religion can come to understand the broader environmental constructions of religious practices and traditions within particular places and times. Paden says, 'Religions do not all inhabit the same world, but actually posit, structure and dwell within a universe that is their own ... All living things select and sense "the way things are" through their own organs and modes of activity' (1994: 51–2). 'Any world' Paden states elsewhere, 'is an open-ended, interactive process, filled with various and complex sensory and cognitive domains, encompassing both representation and practice, both imaginal objects and bodies-in-performance' (2000: 336). Central here are the processes of selection and organisation, of an active, performative ongoing creation of the world. Such language runs uncannily parallel to the language of film production, as each film offers specific geographies, times, languages, personae and is filled with many sensory details (though, unlike religion, they must remain limited to sight and sound and touch), intellectual suggestions, imaginary and 'real' objects and performing bodies.

Worldmaking is actively engaged with the raw materials that make up what is in the strictest sense called the 'earth', but importantly with the entire universe, the cosmos. Religions and films, as varieties of worldmaking enterprises, both do this. On the broadest, most abstract level, worldmaking makes use of the spaces and times that are available in the physical world, significantly incorporating common elements such as earth, air, fire, metal, wood and water. Worldmaking is a performative drama in which humans are the costume designers and liturgists, scriptwriters and sermon givers, cinematographers and saints, projectionists and priests. All the world's a stage and all worlds are stages. The dramatic activity is what humans partake in when we attempt to make meaning of the spaces, times and people that make up our lives. And it is what filmmakers, artists and religious figures offer to this human drama.

How do religions accomplish such worldmaking? Two of religion's most powerful components are myths and rituals, replete with symbols. Symbol-infused myths and rituals create worlds for their adherents who periodically and temporarily participate in these constructed worlds. Significantly, the worlds of myths (whether they concern, for example, the creation of the universe or tell the tale of a great hero) cannot be inhabited directly but can be participated in from time to time through the ritual retelling, re-enacting and remembering of the stories. Christian communion recalls the story of the crucifixion of Jesus Christ, Jewish Passover re-enacts the exodus of the ancient Israelites, Janmashtami celebrates the birth of Lord Krishna, and the Hajj ultimately re-enacts the Prophet Muhammad's triumphant entry into Mecca and his circling of the ancient Arabic shrine, the Kaba. Rituals and myths are intertwined, setting their participants within a world that is simultaneously here and now, just as it is part of an enduring history that fosters identity and belonging.

When we get to analytical descriptions of mythic and ritualistic operations, we begin to see the dramatic nature of worldmaking unfold. Myths and rituals assist in the creation of worlds through activities that frame, exclude, focus, organise and re-present elements of the known world. Anthropologist Mary Douglas speaks to the function of rituals, indirectly noting the power of mythic story: 'A ritual provides a frame. The marked off time or place alerts a special kind of expectancy, just as the oft-repeated "Once upon a time" creates a mood receptive to fantastic tales ... Framing and boxing limit experience, shut in desired themes or shut out intruding ones' (1992: 78). Meanwhile, Paden offers this definition for the function of ritual: 'The basic feature of ritual is its power of focus ... In ritual, what is out of focus is brought into focus. What is implicit is made explicit. All ritual behaviour gains its basic effectiveness by virtue of such undivided, intensified concentration and by bracketing off distraction and interference' (1994: 95–6). Similarly, for myth: Paden claims that it is 'a definitive voice that names the ultimate powers that create, maintain and re-create one's life', and that it works by 'organising and presenting reality in a way that makes humans not just conceivers but respondents and partakers' (1994: 73–4). I am not suggesting these brief examples are comprehensive definitions of these terms but rather introducing the ways myth and ritual participate in the larger process of worldmaking. As should be becoming apparent, myths and rituals operate like films: they utilise techniques of framing, thus including some themes, objects and events while excluding others; and they serve to focus the adherent's attention in ways that invite humans in to the ritualised world in order to become participants.

Worlds are not merely created once and for always, they must be kept going, maintained. From time to time people will see through the constructed nature of the world and ask questions, poking holes in the sacred canopy. So, socio-cultural systems like religion have to continually legitimate the world that has been created. Worldmaking, in other words, is deeply bound to what Peter Berger calls 'world-maintenance'. Because there is a dialectical process between the projected societal views of the cosmos and individual enquiry and creativity, the world must be maintained on a perpetual basis. For reasons that I hope to make clear, I am transposing world-maintenance as 're-creation', in order to get at the dynamic dialectics that Berger, Goodman and Paden highlight. The world is not simply built, but is constantly being maintained through rebuilding, reconstruction, recombining.

The hyphen is injected into re-creation to remind us how to pronounce this word in a way that resonates with its deeper meaning. Modern English has transformed the term into 'recreation', as in 'recreational vehicle' or departments of 'parks and recreation' – something we do to *get away from* the world. Yet at the heart of the idea, even if we forget it, is the activity of creation. Recreation is a way to re-create the world, which often means taking a step back from the world to see how it is put together, if only to figure out how it can be rearranged. On those days of re-creation, the world looks different. We see what we should have seen all along. We remember what is truly important.

That recreation, including moviegoing, occurs on the weekends in the modern world is not accidental. These two days coincide with the Jewish and Christian holy days, when the faithful around the world attend religious services, participate in their 'true' communities and take time to be in touch with their Creator. At least, that's the idea. As the Western world has grown restless with its religiosity, new forms of re-creation have emerged, one of which is, of course, the world of cinema. Indeed, what preacher's sermon can compete with multi-million dollar special effects? What Sabbath meal can steer us away from the possibility that such beautiful people as Julia Roberts and Richard Gere might fall in love? Many priests and pastors are now incorporating film clips into their sermons, creating a multi-mediated spectacle of the Sunday morning worship service.

The Jewish tradition of the Sabbath is particularly insightful as a way to approach the re-creation of the world as it relates to film. 'On the seventh day, God rested', we are told in the mythical language at the beginning of Genesis. But in the next chapter we read that the Creator was not so passive at this time. If religions, in the language of contemporary religious studies, are centered around that which is 'sacred', then the Jewish and Christian traditions would be first and foremost centered around the Sabbath day, for that is the first thing that God blesses and makes holy (Heb. *kadosh*) according to the scriptures: 'God blessed the seventh day and made it holy' (Genesis 2.3). As Abraham Heschel puts it in his classic book on the Sabbath, 'It is a day on which we are called upon to share in what is eternal in time, to turn from the results of creation to the mystery of creation; from the world of creation to the creation of the world' (1951: 10). Contrary to public opinion, the idea of the Sabbath is not one hollowed out by a list of rules and regulations leaving a community in a state of passivity, but rather is an active, vital time. Judaism has a strong tradition of understanding the Sabbath as the *completion* of creation, that on the seventh day God did not refrain from creating as much as God created the Sabbath. The Sabbath, according to this view, is the 'real world', the rest of the week a necessary other world. 'The Sabbath is not for the sake of the weekdays; the weekdays are for the sake of the Sabbath' (1951: 14).[1]

If the Sabbath is the day we turn 'to the mystery of creation' and 'from the world of creation to the creation of the world', then film mimics this very process. Film makes us wonder about the world again, makes us say 'wow!' and offers images that allow us to see things in a new way. This is not to say all film accomplishes this, for there seems to be somewhat of an inverse relation between the spectacular images of film and the capacity for the viewer's imagination – the more dazzling the image, the more depressed the imagination – but then again, the challah bread, the candles, the recitation of prayers, are not foolproof ways to stir our minds and bodies either. At its best, the Sabbath puts people in touch with their Creator, with their family and with the created world. Bobby Alexander defines the aim of religious rituals in general: 'Traditional religious rituals open up ordinary life to ultimate reality or some transcendent being or force in order to tap its transformative power' (1997: 139). At its best, film puts people in touch with the world again in new ways. In both of these, one is connected with their world only by experiencing another world.

To be active consumers and participants in front of the film screen, altar or Sabbath table – in order to maintain the hyphen in re-creation – it is necessary at times to dissect and analyse, to take things apart and then recombine them, as Nelson Goodman suggests. As students of religion and film, we must see, hear, feel and think through the ways these worlds are made and re-created. Such are the goals of religious studies and film studies programmes across the world, and such is the aim of this book.

II. Filmic worldmaking and re-creation

The re-creation of the world is perhaps so obvious in the cinema that we tend to overlook it. In the beginning, every film begins with the production studio's logo. Many of these logos self-consciously demonstrate the ways in which the world is not simply being reflected onscreen, but the way the world is being actively reimagined, and the way cinema functions to relate the *nomos* and *cosmos*. These moving logos continually portray a predominant theme through their scenarios: the heavens and earth are connected through the production of cinema. The logo for Universal depicts a spinning earth, with a thousand points of light appearing across the continents (presumably movie theatres) as the view zooms out to show the whole globe, and the name 'Universal' spins into place as a belt spanning the planet. Dreamworks' logo begins with an image of still water, into which a fishing line is dropped, then the camera moves up to find a boy cradled in the curve of the 'D' as the name hangs, suspended in mid-air and surrounded by clouds, evoking a lunar point of view on the world below. Elsewhere, Warner Brothers displays the 'WB' shield floating amongst the clouds; the now-defunct Orion showed its eponymous stars; and Paramount and Columbia both set their icons so high up on a pedestal that only the clouds and a few other mountain peaks can join them in their pantheon of world imagining.

Through such examples it is clear that film production companies are fully cognisant of the other worlds and ethereal perspectives they provide for their viewers, and gleefully promote these perspectives as they reaffirm a cosmology that evokes a 'looking up' to where the wondrous things are. In this way cinema offers a glimpse of the heavens, of other worlds above and beyond earthly existence, even as these other worlds must be relatable to the visible worlds on earth.

Such posturing is not far from the need for religious worlds to legitimate their worldmaking activity. As Berger suggests 'Religion legitimates social institutions by bestowing upon them an ultimately valid ontological status, that is, by *locating* them within a sacred and cosmic frame of reference ... Probably the most ancient form of this legitimation is the conception of the relationship between society and cosmos as one between microcosm and macrocosm. Everything "here below" has its analogue "up above". By participating in the institutional order men, *ipso facto*, participate in the divine cosmos' (1967: 33–4). Likewise, cinema 'projects' a particular human order onto a screen, promoting its productions as a link between the 'here below' and 'up above' – on mountain tops, in the clouds, encircling the earth. At the same time, the screen is literally created to be *larger than life*. Transcendent of this-worldly concerns, rules or behaviours the cinema enables a god's-eye view of things, even if we have long ago given up the 'heaven above/earth below' cosmic separation.

Filmmakers and theorists, as well as production companies, realise the re-creative activity of film production as well, and they tend to understand worldmaking in terms of *space* and *time*. Siegfried Kracauer, in his *Theory of Film* (originally published in 1960) suggests the spatial significance of the larger-than-life images and the ways in which worlds are remade when projected onscreen: 'Any huge close-up reveals new and unsuspected formations of matter; skin textures are reminiscent of aerial photographs, eyes turn into lakes or volcanic craters. Such images blow up our environment in a double sense: they enlarge it literally; and in doing so, they blast the prison of conventional reality, opening up expanses which we have explored at best in dreams before' (1997: 48).[2] And editor Paul Hirsch connects worldmaking to the temporal dimensions of filmmaking when he claims, 'Film is truth, but it's all an illusion. It's fake. Film is deceptive truth! ... Editing is very interesting and absorbing work because of the illusions you can create. You can span thirty years within an hour and a half. You can stretch a moment in slow motion. You can play with time in extraordinary ways' (1992: 188–9).[3] Through the very technology of film, a new world is assembled – through the camera lens and in the editing room – and then projected onscreen. Viewers see the world, but see it in entirely new ways because everyday perceptions of space and time are altered. Such time and space travel are not foreign to the procedures of religious worldmaking. In fact, if one were to substitute the word 'myth' for 'film' in Hirsch's comment, we would come across a popular definition of myth: 'Telling lies to tell the truth.' And through the re-creation of time and space, we have a world, created anew.

In the 1950s, the aesthetician and film theorist Etienne Souriau made a scientific attempt at distinguishing several layers of 'reality' when dealing with film, and in doing so inadvertently offers some suggestions to religious studies scholars interested in film. These levels are:

1. afilmic reality (the reality that exists independently of filmic reality)
2. profilmic reality (the reality photographed by the camera)
3. filmographic reality (the film as physical object, structured by techniques such as editing)
4. screenic (or filmophanic) reality (the film as projected on a screen)
5. diegetic reality (the fictional story world created by the film; the type of reality 'supposed' by the signification of film)
6. spectatorial reality (the spectator's perception and comprehension of a film)
7. creational reality (the filmmaker's intentions)[4]

I will deal with almost all of these levels throughout this book, though not in any systematic, layer-by-layer way. I note them here to further evidence the multiple layers of reality that one must engage with when dealing with film. It is not enough to encapsulate the narrative arc and suggest some religious implications from a literary perspective; rather, the edited, cinematographic and projected layers of film's re-creation of the world must be taken into account. And while these seven layers are each of individual interest, the full implications simply delimit the more general analogous relations I am attempting here. One could, I suppose, discuss each of these layers in ways that relate to Clifford Geertz's extensive definition of religion, defined as: '(1) a system of symbols which acts to (2) establish powerful, pervasive and long-lasting moods and motivations in men by (3) formulating conceptions of a general order of existence and (4) clothing these conceptions with such an aura of factuality that (5) the moods and motivations seem uniquely realistic' (1973: 90). Souriau's level 2 could relate to Geertz's point 3, Souriau's level 4 could relate to Geertz's point 4, Souriau's level 6 could relate to Geertz's point 5 and so forth. The key point I take from Souriau for now is the general distinction between the profilmic and afilmic realities, the world 'onscreen' and the world 'out there', but also of their mutual implication.

Finally, to bring this theoretical filmic and religious re-creating of the world down to a more concrete level, consider the following brief note on the production of Terry Gilliam's film *Tideland* (2005):

> Terry Gilliam filmed his newest movie, *Tideland*, in Saskatchewan last fall, racing to complete the location shots before winter set in. The Mitch Cullin novel on which the film is based is mostly set in West Texas, but Mr Gilliam had substituted the Canadian prairie instead. The evening after he wrapped, it started to snow, and the cast, crew and director all saw this as an omen...
>
> Most of *Tideland* takes place inside a long-abandoned farmhouse, and the set was a miracle of grunginess and dilapidation in which cobwebs had been applied, brand new walls had been distressed to look old and water-stained, and ancient household implements had been knocked around until they looked even older. But as the camera tracked around and the crew moved props in and out, they accidentally created little pathways of relative orderliness, and Mr Gilliam several times called for more dust. (McGrath 2005)

In the making of film – which is not far from the making of religion – through symbolic representational images, scenarios can be substituted just as afilmic weather encroaches on profilmic realities, and even entropy can be created onscreen. On the flip side, viewers end up seeing this re-created world onscreen, believing in the fiction, because such belief is how we humans survive our everyday life. We go to the cinema and to the temple for recreation, to escape, but we also crave the re-creative aspects, maintaining the canopy of meaning over our individual and social lives as we imagine how the world could be. *What if?*

III. Outline of the book

As already stated, through this book I look at religion and film through the lens of worldmaking. I take this approach because it self-reflectively provides a way to view the world in which humans live, and not just the world as projected onscreen. There are seemingly two (perhaps more) worlds, but those continuously impact each other. Ultimately, it is the points of contact between the worlds that concern me here. The active nature of worldmaking also shifts focus away from mere representational analyses towards the ways entire worlds might be created onscreen and at the altar. By situating the relation of religion and film in the context of worldmaking, it becomes possible to tease out relations between profilmic and afilmic realities, and to regard the ways religions and films exist betwixt and between the two types of reality.

The first part of the book is comprised of two chapters, each discussing the ways the afilmic world is captured and put into the profilmic world. At the same time, the chapters relate the filmic dimensions of *mise-en-scène*, editing and cinematography to the religious dimensions of myth and ritual. Chapter 1 begins with a number of well-known Hollywood productions as the chapter explores the mythological dimensions of films such as *Star Wars* (1977), *The Matrix* (1999), *Big Fish* (2003) and *The Passion of the Christ* (2004), especially noting the re-creation of mythology through formal components of *mise-en-scène*. And since myth is generally something which can only continue its existence through an ongoing performance in ritual, chapter 2 makes note of several lesser-known international films that generate their ritualistic impact through the creative conduits of cinematography and editing. Noting the relations of cinematography to community creation, the first part of the chapter examines *Antonia* (*Antonia's Line*, 1985) examining the ups and downs of camera movements and how vertical-hierarchical social structures are cast in tension with horizontal-egalitarian communities. Turning to the function of editing, Dziga Vertov's *Chelovek s kino-apparatom* (*Man with a Movie Camera*, 1929) and Ron Fricke's *Baraka* (1992) both re-create the world through particular editing techniques.

The second part of this book shifts focus away from film form per se to the ways these forms connect with viewers. The focus is on what happens in the movement from screened film to lived reality. In these final two chapters I suggest how the world onscreen impacts the world offscreen. Chapter 3 examines the screened human body in all its mortality, its protuberances and openness in light of Stan Brakhage's avant-garde film *The Act of Seeing With One's Own Eyes* (1971). In the act of seeing another's body, with one's own embodied vision, mortality is an inescapable problem, and I argue for a peculiar form of 'religious cinematics', whereby the seemingly distant and voyeuristic approach to film collapses into an intimate engagement with one's own body. The final chapter demonstrates how films have, Tom Baxter-like, come down off the screen and infiltrated religious rituals such as weddings and bar/bat mitzvahs. Films not only *represent* rituals, they actively alter the ways traditional rituals are enacted.

Through issues raised in these two parts, I demonstrate the ways that, in the end, there is no simple 'two worlds' view. The relation between afilmic reality and profilmic reality, in the early twenty-first century, cannot be separated. Each has infiltrated the other to such a degree that the layers are indistinguishable.

IV. Towards a critical religious film theory

While meant to introduce readers to a complex relationship between religion and film, my intention through this book is also to begin to chart elements of a *critical religious film theory*. I will not be doing this systematically, but rather through an applied process in the following chapters.

It is *critical* because it closely investigates the structural dimensions of how both films and religions are made. It pays attention to inventive and ideological makings and recreations of the world. It looks deeply into the basic building blocks of worlds, such as time and space, the framing and bracketing off of particular parts of these dimensions and their recreated, projected world onto altar and screen. Through these critical endeavours a second layer of critique takes form: the chapters that follow are unafraid to criticise certain worlds that are unethical whether due to racist, sexist or socially unjust creations. The critical stances may come from either a filmic or religious perspective: sometimes films are critical towards religions because of their sexism (the list here would be enormous, but one that quickly comes to mind is Deepa Mehta's *Water* (2005)), and sometimes religions can be critical of films for their presentation of 'unedifying' activities (many liberal Protestants objected to Mel Gibson's *The Passion of the Christ* for its revelry in violence). A critical religious film theory takes both critiques seriously: the religious and the filmic.

The theory presented is *religious* since one of the primary aims is to demonstrate why religions are so powerful and persuasive, though not from an exclusively rationalist standpoint. Religions are persuasive in part because, to quote Geertz again, they 'clothe' their conceptions with an 'aura of factuality', making their 'moods and motivations seem uniquely realistic'. To create useful understandings and experiences of religion, students of religion need to get out of their own heads to realise the bodily, performative and experiential dimensions that make religion as powerful as it is. Many critiques of religion have appeared recently, with many cogent things to say about the troubles of religious traditions, but they fail on one key score: they almost always perceive religion to be something about intellectual belief in a supernatural deity. *Religion, for better or worse, is vastly more like a film than an intellectual proposition*. It is as much and usually more about the clothing and the aura of factuality than it is about the conceptions themselves. An investigation of film provides more information on the structures of religion than a reading of Immanuel Kant or Blaise Pascal will.[5] Creating a critical approach to religion is not intended to diminish religion, but rather to show its power in human life, and why, in a sense, we should all be students of religion.

The other primary object and mode of investigation is *film*. With regard to film I intend to expose the seemingly secular tactics of film production and show why filmmakers have consistently continued to rely on aesthetic strategies that religions have long relied upon. While it may be cheaper to remake an old story than to write from scratch (borrowing from, say, the *Mahabharata,* as in *The Legend of Bagger Vance* (2000) or the book of Genesis as in *Evan Almighty* (2007)), the underlying fact is that these old stories have staying power. Myths are myths for a reason: they present a fascinating, alternative world to the one that their receivers are presently living in. These other worlds tell of the beginnings of the known world, of the gods and goddesses of this world, or of heroes who inspire contemporary behaviour. To suggest that these old stories are 'untrue' is to deeply miss their authority as presented and perceived. Further, the watching of these mythological stories creates a primal response on the part of the viewers, who throughout the history of the world have responded to such mythological structures by creating performative rituals that re-enact the old stories and make them new again in the present age. The study of film and its reception contributes to the study of religious myth and ritual.

Finally, this is *theory*, in the grand old sense of the term: *theoria*. In the Greek tradition (which is not to say this is the only significant conception for such a term), theory is not disembodied, disinterested investigation, but only possibly understood through participation. Theory is taken on through participation in the theatre and the terms are historically linked.

Theories are grasped in theatres, in audio-visual-corporeal experiences of another world presented to the fully sensing body. The myriad, created worlds are connected *in theory*. One must be an onlooker *and* a participant in both religion and film to understand what is to be presented, and to enter into that other world. The only way to shift from observer to world onscreen/altar is to participate, to take part in the happenings of that other world. What this generally entails is the 'theorist/theatre-viewer' must relinquish control of the dividing line between the world onscreen/altar and the world as it seems to exist in the here and now (to run the risk of trying to pay for dinner with fake money). The suspension of disbelief is vital to grasping the power of film *and* the power of religion. And again, I argue, the power of the one can be usefully understood in light of the power of the other.

1 VISUAL MYTHOLOGISING

The penultimate scene in Tim Burton's *Big Fish* reveals the 'truth' of the tall tales told by Edward Bloom (played by Ewan McGregor and Albert Finney) over the years. To the surprise of his disbelieving son Will (Billy Crudup), as well as the viewers of the film, the scene of Edward's funeral displays how the father's fables actually contained within them a kernel of something true. For the most part, Will, and the viewers, assume he has just made it all up. Early on in the film Edward recalls a story of an ostracised giant who lived in a cave outside of town and who is eventually befriended through Edward's cheerful demeanour. Via camera angles and some computer-generated imagery, the giant, 'Karl' (Matthew McGrory), appears at least twice the size of an average man throughout Edward's retellings, probably at least twelve feet tall. And later on we hear the story of Edward's stint in the army, fighting in the Korean war, where he comes upon the conjoined twins, Jing and Ping (Adai Tai and Arlene Tai), singing for the enemy troops. Then, in the funeral scene at the end of the film, viewers are introduced to Karl through a high-angle shot that gets viewers wondering for a few seconds whether Edward's stories were true, as Karl initially appears very tall indeed. A couple of shots later there is a medium shot with the 'giant' talking to other people, and it is revealed that he is no giant, just an unusually tall man. There was a real Karl, and he was tall, only perhaps not a giant of twelve feet. And a side angle shot of the real twins at first makes it appear they are corporeally connected, but then one of them walks off with another character. Twins? Yes. Conjoined? No.

In *Big Fish*, camera angles make Karl the giant appear much bigger than an average man...

...whereas at the end it is revealed that he was real, but not a giant – just very tall

Big Fish gets us thinking about the power of stories, the power of their fictions and the ways they construct identities and worlds for their tellers and hearers. Furthermore, it gets us thinking about the visual construction of such worlds.[1] Through decidedly visual means, the stories Edward tells in *Big Fish* are both initially exaggerated and eventually brought back down to earth. While verbal narrative is strong throughout the film, there is nothing mentioned verbally about the size of the giant, nor the exact nature of the twins, yet the visual effects of the film display Edward's stories in larger-than-life form. The film is a tribute to storytelling, to the power of the imagination in creating identity, telling the religious-minded viewer a great deal about the importance of myth in the construction of sacred worlds. But it also *shows* a lot about the power of visual mythologising and its contribution to worldmaking.

With such notions in mind, this chapter explores visual mythologising in the form of filmmaking, looking to the ways stories are created in and through the audio-visual medium, with particular attention to what film theorists have termed *mise-en-scène*. Two mythological films, *Star Wars* and *The Matrix*, will both be discussed through attention to a single scene each, as the props, characters, framing, lighting and overall scenario of these scenes offer clues to the mythological structures given in the films as a whole. There will follow an analysis of the ways mythological references operate in film not simply as a part of verbal narrative trajectories, but also through creating a scenario in which carefully placed objects and carefully chosen characters are shown in relationship to each other onscreen, and then offered to viewers to make further relationships. Finally, we will return to larger theoretical questions of the relation between myth and film, with a discussion of Mel Gibson's *The Passion of the Christ*.

I. Myth and film

Woven through this chapter and picked up again in the conclusion, are two corollary questions on the relation of myth and film. Firstly, what does an examination of film lend to the study of religion, specifically its myths? Secondly, how might an understanding of religious myths and world construction challenge film critics and scholars to expand their analyses?

While more complete answers to these questions will emerge through this chapter and chapters to come, I suggest up front that an answer to the first question begins like this: films can show how myths operate beyond their existence as verbal stories, even as many religious studies scholars still tend to believe myths are comprised of words. Rather, myths, like films, are created in and carried out through visual, tactile, olfactory and other sensual modes. A second part of that answer is that myths are always 'mash-ups' (to borrow some contemporary multi-mediated language), always assembled through bits, pieces and found objects that have been borrowed, begged, stolen and improvised. Film has been and continues to be a natural medium for 'mash-ups' due to its multimedia origins in theatre, photography and focus on everyday life (employees leaving the factory in the Lumières' *La Sortie des usines Lumière* (*Workers Leaving the Lumière Factory*, 1895) and so forth). Meanwhile, attention to the sources of films suggests something about the sources of myths as well.

The start of an answer to the second question would be this: thousands of years and thousands of cultural locations have provided contemporary filmmakers with a storehouse of grand stories that are endlessly adaptable into the audio-visual medium of film. Because myths are inevitably 'mash-ups', directors and screenwriters can cull from stories told through the ages, and often told again in ever-new forms. To miss the begging, borrowing and stealing that mythmakers/filmmakers do is to miss the compulsions of filmmaking in general to create new stories often by retelling old ones. And to deny the mythological origins of so many contemporary films is to risk denying something of the very humanity in the films as well. Unless film theorists and critics understand the power of myth, they will not understand the full power of film.

Myths are, among other things, stories based on real-life events that are extended, enlarged, engorged and riffed on as they are retold, like the tale of the fish that got away and every time the story is retold that fish keeps getting bigger and bigger. The moral of the big fish story is that we are all susceptible to the exaggerations of the storyteller if we were not there to witness it first-hand, and the story does not work if the fish were actually caught – for that would supply tangible and scientific proof. Myth does not deal in scientifically verifiable proofs, which is why ancients and moderns alike have found a weakness in myth, but this is also precisely the point at which myth receives its power. It becomes 'true' because it is told and because it is believed.

There is no space to go into an extensive definition of myth here, nor is it necessary for my interests. As a straightforward articulation by the historian of religions, Wendy Doniger, suggests, a myth 'is a story that is sacred to and shared by a group of people who find their most important meanings in it; it is a story believed to have been composed in the past about an event in the past, or, more rarely, in the future, an event that continues to have meaning in the present because it is remembered' (1998: 2).[2] What is important to me, as for Doniger, is that a definition of myth must deal with the ways myths *function*, how they do what they do and how they do them to people. In the following, these ideas will be drawn upon and then supplemented with a critical religious film theory that adjusts definitions of myth based on an interaction with film.

In light of these initial definitions of myth, *Big Fish* is not just a mundane story about a fish. It goes to great lengths to approximate something larger, and that is a *cosmogony*, a myth about the creation of a world. The opening shots are from under water, with fish swimming across the screen and eventually the 'big fish' makes its way across the film frame. In this way it mimics creation stories from around the world: the Babylonian *Enuma Elish* begins within water associated with *chaos*; and the chaotic waters play a critical role, for instance, in the Iroquouis creation story of the 'woman who fell to earth', as well as the Jewish-Christian account found in Genesis One: 'the earth was a formless void and darkness covered the face of the deep, while a wind [the spirit] from God swept over the face of the waters' (Genesis 1.2). The eponymous fish is, in many senses, Edward's wife Sandra (Jessica Lange) as, according to his stories, she is caught with the glint of his wedding ring; meanwhile Edward ultimately catches (and soon releases) the fish on the day his son Will is born. Throughout the film, Edward's fish stories are the stories of *his* world, beginning with the creation of his world (his wife and son) and ending with his own death. Even so, as Will begins to live in to the stories by participating in the myths himself at his father's deathbed, he realises that the stories are what make him, and all of us, immortal. Edward Bloom helped create his world and with it created a living cosmogony for his family. In learning to believe the stories, his son Will learns something about himself, who he is, where he has come from and ably carries on the tradition to his children, as evidenced in the final scene. Myths may be fictions, but they are believed to be true in a deeper sense than historical investigations can provide.

Myths are powerful not just as cosmogonies, not just answering questions about *where* we come from, but also powerful because they supply answers to questions about *who* we should be. Prominent among such mythologies are hero myths, stories about individuals who have a world taken away from them and then they battle back, often going on great and extensive journeys to do so and emerging triumphant (though it is often a paradoxical view of triumph) in the face of adversity. *Big Fish* is more or less a hero myth. Intriguingly, though there is little space to explore the topic here, it appears that the vast majority of animated films, from Walt Disney productions to Japanese *anime*, seem to find their basic narrative structure in hero mythologies. From *Pinocchio* (1940) to *Shrek* (2001), *Princess Mononoke* (1997) to *Finding Nemo* (2003), there is something deeply understood in the otherworldly (here, animated) realm of heroes. Perhaps it has to do with a normative conception of what should be 'children's stories', something inspiring and that might be aspired to. In this way, a hero myth fosters a sense of identity, of who one might be and of the ethics and therefore choices one must consider to become such. And in this way we quickly slip into the realm of ideology, to which mythology is closely linked. We shall return to this connection later.

II. Myth and mise-en-scène: the matrix and star wars

A careful look at two scenes from the beginnings of two masterfully mythical films sheds light on the ways mythologies are depicted in non-narrative, non-verbal ways. Through a staged and shot scenario, myths are triggered, brought to life. *Mise-en-scène*, briefly put, refers to everything that is seen inside the frame of the film: decoration, props, lighting, costume, colours and figures, as well as how the scenario in general is staged in relation to the camera frame.[3] Film sets are created spaces, and every object and visual orientation, every costume and colour that the viewer sees onscreen is the result of a highly considered process on the part of directors, cinematographers, production designers and others. Props have meanings as much as the words spoken by main characters, and camera angles can express cosmic significance.

Star Wars (that is, the original, also known as 'Episode IV', written and directed by George Lucas, 1977) and *The Matrix* (written and directed by Andy and Larry Wachowski, 1999) are arguably two of the greatest mythological films of all time. They mix and merge cosmogonies and hero myths in multiple ways as they emerge with brand new mythologies that continue into the twenty-first century. The writers and directors of each film self-consciously incorporate the myths of multiple religious traditions into their re-created worlds. While plenty of people have commented on the narrative similarities between both films and the older verbal myths from Buddhist, Taoist, Christian and other traditions, the following examinations pay attention to the ways the audio-visual components of film also re-construct those myths, offering re-created worlds for their viewing, listening audience.[4] My arguments here only touch on the larger narrative of each film, but instead hone in on one scene in each, demonstrating how much can be contained audio-visually in two or three minutes of film-making.

Star Wars: cosmos vs chaos

After the production company credits – here an animated view of the logo of 20th Century Fox rising like a mega-skyscraper above the Hollywood sky-line – *Star Wars* shows a black screen with the simple and now well-known phrase, 'A long time ago, in a galaxy far, far away...'. Immediately we are ush-ered into the realm of myth. Compare this introduction with Genesis 1.1: 'In the beginning, God created the heavens and the earth.' In each rendering we are given the standard deployments of narrative introductions: at the start of a story one should provide the setting, in terms of time and place. The audi-ence has to know where and when the world is that they are observing.

Here myths function parallel to the narratives involved in fictional stories, as well as the psychoanalytic process of identity formation. As already quoted in the introduction, anthropologist Mary Douglas brings such connections together: 'A ritual provides a frame. The marked off time or place alerts a special kind of expectancy, just as the oft-repeated "Once upon a time" creates a mood receptive to fantastic tales' (1992: 78). The beginning of *Star Wars*, as Lucas, 20th Century Fox and others know, introduces viewers to another world, a 'marked off time or place' inducing the audience to expect something fantastic. Intriguingly, and critical to the personal connections involved with mythology, Douglas goes on to quote Marion Milner's research into child psychoanalysis in relation to 'framing': 'the frame marks off the different kind of reality that is within it from that which is outside it; but a temporal-spatial frame marks off the special kind of reality of a psychoanalytic session ... makes possible the creative illu-sion called transference' (in Douglas 1992: 78). Like mythology and ritual, like the psychoanalytic session itself, the filmic manifestation in viewers' minds offers another world. That other world is accessible as one crosses the bordering frame between one world and the next, making possible the 'creative illusion called transference'. Myths, like psychoanalysis, do not work unless some sort of transference occurs, some groups and individuals believe the stories to be true and allow them to affect their lives.

Yet, what initially sets *Star Wars* apart from films about more everyday life, and what begins to set myths apart from regular stories, is the ambiguity provided in its setting. The time and place are given, and yet they are not specific. There is no '14 April 1832' given here. Instead, it is 'A long time ago...'. But, how long is long? To a palaeontologist two million years might be a long time. To my two-year-old daughter five minutes seems an eternity. Genesis's 'In the beginning...' is likewise vague. When, exactly, was the beginning? Beginning of what? And the same is true for the spatial setting: '... a galaxy far, far away'; or in Genesis, it is essentially 'space' that is in the process of being created, when 'God was creating the heavens and earth'. In other words, myths provide a built-in ambiguity that makes them applicable to a variety of people in a variety of times and places. George Lucas understands this, and inscribes it in the beginning of his film, turning a science fiction story (most of which begin with precise dates) into something mythical. Lucas's 'time' is further confounded by the fact that most science fiction films take place in the future, they deal with technology beyond our present day, but here he is setting it in the past. *Star Wars* looks futuristic, but we are told this has already occurred.

Like all stories, myths begin with and are framed by a setting in time and space. Films achieve a similar effect in audio-visual ways through what are known as 'establishing shots', usually long (or extreme long) shots that show the viewer a general setting. Standard Hollywood films might show a large image of a city (the Manhattan skyline shot from across the East River; Chicago with its John Hancock Tower; London with the Houses of Parliament), and then slowly zoom or cut in to more and more local places until reaching the main character's location within the city; and visual clues along the way (automobiles, clothing or hair styles) tell of the temporal period.

In *Star Wars*, the establishing shot that follows the beginning provides a further introduction to the mythic structures of the film, and indicates why it is not just another film about boy-meets-girl and/or good guys vs bad guys. The shot is set in outer space, with nothing but stars dotting an otherwise black sky – no planets or anything else to give us an initial grounding. Immediately thereafter, the title 'STAR WARS' appears onscreen accompanied by a blast of orchestral music (by John Williams).

The audience is jolted, excited by what is to come. As the triumphant, heavily-percussive music continues, a prologue scrolls up the screen, further setting up details of what has happened and what is to come. Viewers are caught up in the narrative, thrust into the middle of action through these words and music.

But the grander mythical cues come just as the words scroll up the screen and disappear into the ether. At that precise instant the jubilant music also all but disappears, leaving only a solo flute playing alongside chimes. For five seconds there is utter calm: the heavens are in their place, the music plays softly, soothingly; there is a cosmic order to the universe. But all we are allowed is five seconds, then the camera, which has been stationary until now, tilts down to reveal an blue/orange-hued planet below, with other planets visible in the distance. During this camera movement, violin strings frantically rise up and the percussion crashes just as two space ships are caught in battle, firing laser guns at each other. Chaos erupts into the cosmos, wars emerge in the midst of stars.

By setting up the establishing shot in outer space, by suggesting an ordered calm to a universe and then introducing chaotic elements, Lucas triggers many elements common in cosmogonies: in the beginning, chaos and cosmos are in battle. In myths as diverse as the Hebrew, Iroquois, Babylonian and Greek creation stories, the grand struggle in their 'establishing shots' is that of cosmos vs chaos. And through history, such myths indicate, this battle perpetually remains just below the surface of things as humans (or other volitional, sentient creatures) enter into this struggle, creating their own *nomic* order. *Star Wars*, writ large, is about stars and wars, cosmos and chaos, and then about relating the human social order to the cosmic order. Through the six episodes of *Star Wars* (1977–2005) there are conflicts, political wagers and power struggles, as protagonists and antagonists battle to retain authority over the social order, continually rooting claims in the cosmic structures around: republicans, democrats, federalists and monarchists can all be found, as can the 'other' spiritual realm of the Jedi Knights. (Another key visual clue relating the cosmos to the nomos happens halfway through the original film, when Luke (Mark Hamill) returns to his home to find his family slaughtered. He stares off at the dual suns about to set over his home planet of Tatooine, and there makes his decision to accept what George Lucas's intellectual mentor Joseph Campbell (1991) called the 'hero's adventure'.)

In the beginning, visually and mythologically, all the remaining ten-plus hours of the *Star Wars* films are set up within the few seconds of the establishing shot in the first film. The film announces itself as far more than a space-age story, and instead tells us that these wars are the wars of all humankind; which is to say it is no less ambitious than a myth.

The Matrix: mythical postmodern pastiche

The second scene of the science fiction masterpiece *The Matrix* introduces us to a strange hermit-prophet-hero called 'Neo', aka Thomas Anderson (played by Keanu Reeves). Much has been written on the connections the film has to Buddhism and Christianity (especially in its Gnostic guise – see Gordon 1995; Lyden 2000; Flannery-Dailey & Wagner 2001), and while these theological/doctrinal analyses are interesting, the discussion here will again aim to point out the visual portrayal of the differing mythical worlds that are created onscreen, and all this within the first three minutes of the film.

The character Trinity (Carrie-Anne Moss) is introduced in the first scene, donning a tight black, shiny outfit and performing martial arts feats that leave a trail of police officers down. There is much to be said here about the *mise-en-scène*, including her clothing and the fact that she is introduced sitting at her computer terminal in a ramshackle hotel room, number 303. The scene is action-packed, with fast-paced music, stunning special effects, gunfights and superheroic hand-to-hand combat, including Trinity's vertical running up walls and leaping from rooftop to rooftop across a city street some twenty or so floors below. The viewer is left amazed but confused as to how all this can happen in the 'real world', especially since the first shot is of Trinity's computer screen with green display characters that tell us the date: '2-19-1998'. Not long into the film we realise again the ambiguous settings of myths whereby the actual date is an illusion and the 'real date' is something unknown; it is probably one hundred years later than people perceive, but no one really knows. This is an apocalyptic myth, foretelling the potential end of the world. Just as the beginnings of worlds are ambiguous, so are the ends.

The action of scene one, centered on Trinity in room 303, gives way to scene two, introducing viewers to Neo who is sprawled across his desk in his apartment, room 101. (At the climax of the film, Neo will re-enter the original room 303, where fate seems to get the better of him and Trinity will bring him back to life.) Neo's apartment is nothing short of a 'cave', dark, dank and dreary.[5] As with Trinity in scene one, we initially meet Neo through his green-tinted computer screen. (The entire film, including the Warner Brothers logo at the beginning, is green-tinted, suggesting something of a fecund, or possibly fetid worldview.) Neo sleeps as his computer performs a search for one 'Morpheus', and international news bulletins flash across the screen, illuminating Neo's face. The searching abruptly stops to show a blank screen, while the words 'Wake up, Neo...' scrawl across it. And Neo does so. As if in Instant Messenger mode, Neo's computer screen tells him to 'Follow the white rabbit', and then predicts a real knock at his real door. All this time, Neo is shot from behind his computer, as he faces the screen in front, and the screen provides his only lighting. The effect is a standard filmic trick of lighting and character development: half of his face is lit, the other half obscured in the dark. He is two people, divided within himself.

The knocked-on door opens to several people obviously looking to have a good time. They also wear black leather and rubber clothing, similar to Trinity's clothing in the previous scene. They pay Neo some money through a slightly opened door, and he goes and finds a special computer disk. We never find out what is on the disk, but we are led to believe the computer program is not strikingly different from hallucinogenic drugs. The lead male takes the disk from Neo and exclaims, 'Hallelujah! You're my saviour, man! My own personal Jesus Christ!' The man takes a look at Neo's pale complexion and dour face and suggests Neo needs to get out a bit more, get a little 'R&R'. He turns to his companion 'Dujour' who happens to have a white rabbit tattooed on her shoulder. Neo recognises the tattoo as the sign given through his computer, and hence follows, Alice-like, down the rabbit hole. The hole gets grander and more upside-down as the film continues.

As Neo walks around his dark apartment in this early scene, the viewer continues to find clues to the myriad myths that are strewn throughout the film. The *chiaroscuro* lighting effect reveals several stations of a windowless space. The computer disk for the partygoers is found in a book entitled *Simulacra and Simulation*. For those raised on postmodern theory, this will be recognised as a collection of essays from the French sociologist, Jean Baudrillard. Neo opens it and it is revealed to be a simulated book, with carved-out pages that offer a hidden storage space, much like

In *The Matrix*, 'Neo' is introduced in his room, 101, as the lighting shows him to be a divided person

we see in other movies with guns or bottles of whisky in the centre. The hollowed-out part that contains the special stash comes in the middle of a piece entitled 'On Nihilism', which is Baudrillard's essay on Friedrich Nietzsche and his atheism. In the late nineteenth century Nietzsche told us God was dead, but in the new world of 'simulated transparency', Baudrillard suggests, 'God is not dead, he has become hyperreal' (1994: 159). Relatedly, in a single essay entitled 'Simulacra and Simulation', Baudrillard offers his postmodern inversion of Plato's allegory of the cave, in which there are successive stages of the image. In the beginning, an image, as a referent, is a reflection of a basic reality (this is what religious icons around the world are based upon). But eventually that grounding in reality disappears and is swallowed by the ubiquity of the image itself in a mass-mediated society, leading to the final stage in which the image 'bears no relation to any reality whatever: it is its own pure simulacrum' (1988: 170).[6] Due to the prominence of mass media in our lives, we can no longer claim anything to be more real than anything else, including the gods and goddesses. (The character Morpheus will even quote Baudrillard later in the film as he introduces Neo to the Matrix, saying, 'Welcome, to the desert of the Real' (1994: 166).) *The Matrix* as a whole is premised on a 'two worlds' view, in which the simulated world appears to be the 'real world', but is in fact a computer program. As Hindu sages, the Buddha and the Gnostics claimed millennia ago, our perceived world is an illusion, *maya*.

So, in approximately three minutes of edited time at the start of *The Matrix* we find reference to myriad mythologies, both religious and secular, ancient and postmodern: from ancient philosophy (Plato's allegory of the cave) to postmodern inversions of it (Baudrillard's simulacra), from nineteenth-century fantastical tales (Lewis Carroll's *Through the Looking Glass* (1871), *à la* the white rabbit) to the larger religious prophetic figures of Jesus Christ and the Buddha. Neo as Jesus Christ the Saviour is invoked through the conversation at the door, but also through his continually-referenced anagram as the 'one'. In the third instalment of *The Matrix* (*The Matrix Revolutions*, 2003) Neo sacrifices himself, with arms in cruciform, as a character functioning as a *deus ex machina* speaks, 'It is done', referencing the last words of Jesus Christ in the Christian gospels. The Christic-redemptive dimensions are fairly obvious to anyone growing up in and familiar with Western and/or Christian cultures, and little more needs to be said here.

Neo's other prophetic incantation as the Buddha is suggested through the first words addressed to him, 'Wake up, Neo...'. The literal translation of the 'Buddha' is the one who has awoken ('enlightenment' is an abstraction of a more primary metaphor of waking from sleep). Further, Neo's comments to the partygoers at his apartment door are: 'You ever have the feeling that you're not sure if you're awake or still dreaming?' Meanwhile, the final song of the film is entitled 'Wake Up' (by Rage Against the Machine) and dream references abound in the film (for example, 'Morpheus' is the Greek mythological name of the god of dreams and the dreamworld). Indeed, Neo, Morpheus, Trinity and others function as *bodhisattvas*, beings who have achieved enlightenment, meanwhile postponing it, in order to help others to see through this illusory life.

And this is where the leather/rubber clothing worn by people in the 'matrix' itself is more than a fashion statement. Throughout the film, when characters enter the 'false' world of the matrix, they usually wear leather. Such clothing is 'second skin', which takes on two connotations. Firstly, the clothing is itself taken from another animal (typically a cow), so that leather clothing is skin on skin. Also, as skin it stretches and curves, so while providing a surface coating to one's actual body, it both shows the contours of the body as it simultaneously hides the body; it reveals and conceals at the same time. Its existence functions on a level of simulation, as second skins extend the two worlds narrative emphasis of the film. Just as the bodies walking around inside the matrix are residual self-images of the real bodies of the people in the pods, so the second skins worn by the characters reinforce the simulated bodies.

In the end, what we find is that *The Matrix*, like *Star Wars*, is a contemporary mythological story that combines multiple myths from multiple traditions. And while this may be construed as a critique of the postmodern age, with its predilection towards pastiche, it is also concomitant with myths throughout the world and at all times. All myths are pastiches; all myths borrow from previous myths in order to construct something new. As James Ford (2000) suggests in the midst of a survey of *The Matrix*, 'Myths are constantly adapted to new cultural contexts and worldly realities.' Originality is not the key to mythic tellings; rather, what is important is a unique way of combining old forms in new fashions. Films such as *Star Wars* and *The Matrix* have performed the function of reintroducing the power of myth for our contemporary lives, and they succeed precisely because they have borrowed from the powerful themes, ideas, symbols and narratives of myths through the ages. They do this in verbal dialogue as well as through a careful use of visual symbols, including props, costume and camera angles.

III. Worldmaking and filmmaking: an ideological warning

There is much more to say about *Star Wars* and *The Matrix* in relation to mythology and, as noted earlier, many have done so before. In relation to *Star Wars* this includes the hero's journey undertaken by Luke Skywalker, or the grand Tao-like opposing energies of 'the Force' used by the black-clothed Darth Vader and the white-clothed Skywalker. For *The Matrix* the further mythic relations would include comment on the place of 'Zion' as the longed-for place of return from exile, the role of 'Thomas' Anderson (the Syriac roots of Thomas are related to a 'twin', just as the Gnostic Gospel of Thomas plays on this relation of Jesus and Thomas), and Morpheus playing the role of the pagan lord of the dreamworld. But before suggesting mythologies are simply positive things to let into our lives, or before offering a neat conclusive interpretation, I end with an ideological critique of the mythology brought forth in the *mise-en-scène* of *The Matrix*.

In scene three of the film, Neo and Trinity meet amidst the leather-and rubber-clad partygoers in a nightclub, and make a connection that lasts through the following films. This initial meeting begins the journey of 'waking up' for Neo, as Trinity helps to clue him in to the way the world actually works. Because we have seen how these two characters are introduced in the opening scenes of *The Matrix*, let us turn to a later framing of them. At the beginning of the film we find a strong white female character, Trinity, and a strong black male character, Morpheus (Laurence Fishburne). Trinity and Morpheus are both insiders to the matrix, with a lot of knowledge about the reality of the two worlds; we can say that they are enlightened. Neo, the good-looking white male, is not enlightened, at least not initially, and the first half of the movie demonstrates his profound ignorance. He is eventually enlightened, understanding and experiencing the truth of the two worlds created by the matrix, but it takes some time – through most of the film he is far behind the other characters, like Morpheus and Trinity, in knowledge and understanding.

Nonetheless, the climactic scene, in which Agent Smith (Hugo Weaving) seemingly kills Neo, demonstrates another prominent mythology that filters through this film: the Hollywood myth of white-supremacist romantic relationships. Just as the Wachowski brothers pull on a variety of myths to create a new, hybrid telling of myth, they also refer to Hollywood, which as a whole has become a serious contender for creating the most prominent mythologies of the contemporary age. Thus, what we see through *The Matrix* is a hybridising of mythologies, most prominently Christian and Buddhist. Yet, what prevails over both these traditions in the end is the Hollywood myth of white, heterosexual relations between good-looking people.

As Neo is killed in the matrix, his 'real' body also undergoes a death. His body is framed by the camera; he lies back in his chair with his brain jacked in to the matrix, and Trinity looks lovingly upon him. He dies in both worlds, but Trinity comes down upon him like a spirit and kisses him. The couple's kiss is framed with what appear to be fireworks behind them (actually the evil 'sentinels' trying to break in with laser weapons). This kiss restores life to Neo: he is resurrected, with obvious Christic allusions. Yet after all the special effects, all the new and original ways of telling old stories, *The Matrix* relies on the familiar Hollywood scenario – in which good-looking white male and good-looking white female kiss at the end of the film in the rain/under fireworks/in the midst of chaos in general. Just when we were sure that a strong white woman or a strong black male might

The Matrix ends like many Hollywood films, with a good-looking white woman kissing a good-looking white man, under the stars/rain/fireworks

take the lead, in the end these characters are simply props for the good-looking white male, who plays the role of the Saviour, the Buddha, The One. This does not deny the strength Trinity or Morpheus display through the film, but as the trilogy of films move on it becomes more and more clear that all others are there to make way for Neo's heroic journey to save the world. This hero's adventure, centred on Neo, provides the basis for all that follows in the sequels.

In *The Matrix*, as in religion, ideology is deeply implicated with mythology; they are inextricable. Yet this link should not stop anyone from considering myth as critically important for the creation and maintenance of human worlds. It is naïve to suggest they are separate, and equally naïve to think one can be understood without the other. Instead, I am sympathetic to the French playwright/poet/theorist Hélène Cixous, when she considers, in language appropriate to the mythology of *The Matrix*, 'For me ideology is a kind of vast membrane enveloping everything. We have to know that this skin exists even if it encloses us like a net or like closed eyelids' (1986: 145). Yet, she continues, 'we have to know that, to change the world, we must constantly try to scratch and tear it. We can never rip the whole thing off, but we must never let it stick or stop being suspicious of it. It grows back and you start again' (ibid.). Cixous' challenge is part of the challenge proposed in the introduction of this book for a 'critical religious film theory' which would create critical responses to the representations of religion in film and to worlds constructed on film.

Conclusion

At the beginning of this chapter, I suggested two corollary questions that form the basis of my filmic analyses in relation to myth. The first had to do with rethinking myth in light of film. The second was the other way around: how an understanding of film might be rethought based on what we know about the ways myths operate. Throughout this chapter, in examining a couple of films, we have seen the ways in which some filmmakers utilise elements of *mise-en-scène* to tell a mythical story in visual form. Sometimes that visual form reaffirms the verbal story, sometimes extends it and sometimes hints at worlds alternate to those created merely through words. On the other hand, this chapter has also tried to show how understanding the power of mythical stories and how they function in humans' lives might offer something to the student of film, suggesting some of the reasons myths are powerful on a humanistic level.

Films, like the ones discussed here, are a blending of mythologies. Their existence as a 'mash-up' is indicative of what all religious myths are about: begging, borrowing and stealing. This is part of what gives them such great power to affect people's lives. Throughout history myths have been created by borrowing other cultures' myths, setting differing mythologies alongside each other, and then honing the story down into a new package that becomes identified with an emerging community. Rip. Mix. Burn. Christianity takes the mythologies and rituals surrounding the Jewish Passover – Jesus was Jewish and the 'last supper' was a Passover meal – and turns it into the thoroughly Christian activity of Communion. Just as the Jewish Passover is focused on remembrance of liberation in the form of the exodus out of Egyptian slavery, so does the Christian Communion centre on remembrance of the body and blood of Christ as the path to liberation, but for a distinct community and for distinct purposes.

Contemporary films have tapped into this power and will continue to do so. Why write a new story when ancient mythologies provide thousands of pages of wonderful tales to take inspiration from? Filmmakers, like all artists, beg, borrow and steal from various sources to produce a final artwork. The resulting framed and edited series of images and sounds is both unique and *un*-original: the juxtapositions may be unique, but the individual pieces are borrowed and it has all been said before. This is not in any way to diminish the role of the artist in society, but to recast it, freeing it from its roots in the Romantic/Christian traditions that conceive of art being created *ex nihilo*, out of nothing.

Meanwhile, students of religious and film studies have to walk that careful line between praising the great imaginative stories of old and paying attention to the subtle ways these stories might maintain oppressive systems of power. Often, the individual components that are 'mashed up' are not put on the same playing field, so that one mythological structure emerges as prominent and attention needs to be drawn there, as is the case with *The Matrix*.

The begging and borrowing also cuts across media. In so doing film productions point out how myths operate in multi-mediated ways. Mel Gibson's *The Passion of the Christ* highlights this point, though I do not want to devote too much time to something for which as much ink has been spilled as fake blood in the film. *The Passion of the Christ* is a mythical, multi-mediated 'mash-up' *par excellence*. For the film Gibson drew on a millennium's worth of Passion plays, The Stations of the Cross, the writings of nineteenth-century (anti-Semitic and possibly insane) mystic Anne Catherine Emmerich (channelled through Clemens Brentano), Renaissance and Baroque painting (especially from Rembrandt and Caravaggio), the New Testament gospels, some brief historical scholarship, a century's worth of 'Jesus films' (from early works on the life and passion of Jesus to Sidney Olcott's *From the Manger to the Cross* (1911) to *King of Kings* (1927) and Martin Scorsese's *The Last Temptation of Christ* from 1988) and from the genre of horror films: the *mise-en-scène* of the first sequence is ripped from the filmmaking styles of John Carpenter or Wes Craven – spooky garden, fog machines rolling, creepy hooded figure with snake. These elements make us think that we just know someone is going to die.[7]

Some of the sources of Gibson's film are noted here for two reasons. Firstly, to suggest that it is not a 'historically accurate' account of the last hours of Jesus of Nazareth, in spite of what some have suggested, but is another mythological 'mash-up'. Secondly, visual mythologising involves multi-mediated mixings. The sources are sometimes literary, but just as often come from painting, sculpture, photography and drama, as well as a history of cinema. Likewise, myths are also multi-mediated.

The beginning of *The Passion of the Christ* looks like a slasher film: the full moon, fog and trees suggest impending death

The deeper implication of this chapter is that, for a religious study of cinema, films are not simply verbal narratives. They create and re-create the world through colour, form, design, symbols, movement and music. My suggestions here, while brief, can be used in a variety of ways in the religious studies classroom. By beginning with the human body, with all its sensual perceptions, as a basis for interaction with persons and a central conduit for religious life, religious studies might take a cue from film studies by observing the visual and acoustic (and bodily in general) ways humans participate in the process of worldmaking. That myths might be *seen* as well as *heard* is not unusual within religions. Navajo sand paintings, Tibetan *thangkas* and Japanese gardens are all visual, material modes of mythologising. Such imagistic objects spatialise sacred stories, give them body, allow them to be interacted with through human bodies and their sense organs. Films remind us that myths are not meant to be intellectual, cerebral exercises, but embodied. Thus we come close to the realm of ritual, taken up in the next chapter.

The general argument being made here is that films function formally like religions.[8] They are structured in similar ways through their mutual re-creations of space and time. This re-creation is then projected outward (externalised), making it appear, as Clifford Geertz might say, 'uniquely realistic' (1973: 90). In this way these audio-visual, experiential stories impact human lives, offering models for living, not just cerebrally, but through the body. This means that religious studies students need to pay attention to what is uniquely filmic about film and, by extension, that our lives as humans are constructed through the sights and sounds and smells that surround us. Meanwhile, some sights and smells are more persuasive then others, challenging us to live differently, which might have both positive and negative effects.

2   RITUALISING FILM IN SPACE AND TIME

The opening shots of David Lynch's *Blue Velvet* (1986) introduce an orderly world created through vertical and horizontal spatial dimensions and primary colours. The first shot is of the sky, blue with scattered clouds, as the camera tilts down to a white picket fence. Eventually red tulips appear against the white fence with blue sky in the background. The larger themes of the film could have a universal relevance, and yet Lynch makes clear that this is the United States, as the red, white and blue composition of the first shot is extended by the proverbial white picket fences of American suburbia. The next few shots are edited so as to alternate between horizontal and vertical spatial orientations. Red, white, blue and yellow colours dominate, while mundane, neighbourhood images of fire trucks and crosswalks appear. The viewer is eventually brought inside, to a living room where a woman sits sipping coffee while watching television. It seems like a beautiful day until we see what she is watching: a black-and-white close-up image of a man's hand holding a revolver. This is the first subtle disturbance in the so-far cosmically ordered world – not much, but enough to knock the neat and tidy perspective off-kilter. The next images take us back outside to a man – later revealed to be the protagonist's father, Mr Beaumont (Jack Harvey) – watering his garden, just as strange noises begin to emerge from the water spigot. A kink in the hose halts the water flow and while the man attempts to untangle it he suffers a stroke. The camera then resumes its downward tilt, this time passing below Mr Beaumont – who is now lying on the grass with water still spurting out of the phallic hose as a dog attempts to drink it – delving into the earth below. Here the creepy-crawly domain of bugs and insects are revealed to be scampering over each other, all of which is reinforced by an eerie soundtrack, making the viewer feel as if they are truly in that very underworld. The remainder of the film continues with such foreboding imagery (see Drazin 1999).

Blue Velvet imagistically begins with revelations of a world similar to that revealed in the opening shots of *Star Wars*: cosmos above, chaos below. In this way, these two films present worlds both radically new and entirely ancient; in this most modern of visual media we find filmmakers relying on primeval cosmologies where peace and harmony exist *above* and chaos subsists *below*. Yet, rather than leaving us in the mythically distant 'long time ago and far, far away', *Blue Velvet* brings the cosmos down to earth, to our neighbourhood, connecting up with the mundane tasks of watering the lawn, going to school and watching television. And then it unveils the chaos that lies under the very ground on which we walk. The macrocosm is transplanted into the microcosm, the world out there is remade into the here and now.

This chapter connects one of the most crucial elements of religion, namely ritual, to two of the most crucial dimensions of filmmaking, namely cinematography and editing (though as already hinted at, *mise-en-scène* continues to be important). *Blue Velvet* shows, at least in one sense, what rituals are capable of doing: bringing the cosmos into the present space and time, allowing people to interact with the alternative, religiously-constructed world and often to re-enact the myths that help establish those world structures. I am not suggesting that the cinematography and *mise-en-scène* of *Blue Velvet* are themselves rituals, but that the film's formal structures are akin to the formal structures of ritual.

Attention is again set on specific scenes from films. Because a critical religious film theory takes the structures of films and religions as part of its focus, this chapter pays attention to segments of films, specific shots or scenes that simultaneously function metonymically to reveal something about the larger narratives of films. After a brief theoretical section relating ritual and film more generally, the second part of the chapter pays attention to *space in relation to cinematography*, while the third part takes up the structural element of *time in relation to editing*. The second part explores films that hone in on community and the ways they are constructed in space, especially focusing on Marleen Gorris's *Antonia* (*Antonia's Line*, 1995). In these films, community is represented through cinematographic devices.

What they rely on is a strong sense of horizontally ordered space, as opposed to vertical dimensions, to produce sacred communities and those differing dimensions are bound up with gender. The third part of the chapter turns especially to Ron Fricke's *Baraka*, while also refering back to Dziga Vertov's *Man With a Movie Camera*. Each operates similarly, without characters or dialogue, instead re-creating the world through the chronological displacements and spatial connections that editing allows. Meanwhile, the aims of each can be easily differentiated: one praises the worker and Soviet society in a fairly specific locale, the other praises a nebulous 'spirituality' found all around the world. In both, editing becomes the everyday elixir that makes the movies, and that ultimately produces something sacred.

I. Ritual and film

As with the previous chapter, this one is framed by two intersecting sets of questions: what does a study of the forms and functions of rituals tell us about the ways films are created? And, conversely, what does an examination of filmmaking uncover about the aesthetical impulses behind rituals? Partial answers are unfolded throughout the following and returned to in the conclusion of this chapter.

Definitions of rituals can be found throughout a great deal of literature on the subject and this is not the place to work out or through the differences. We have already had a few excerpts of definitions in the previous chapters from scholars like Barbara Myerhoff, Mary Douglas and William Paden, who have emphasised the abilities of ritual to frame, select and focus. In the chapters that follow this one, we will see a few more definitions, but for the sake of present simplicity, we have here what I understand to be a useful, pragmatic definition, especially with regard to the 'two worlds' argument made earlier. Bobby Alexander, the anthropologist of religion, suggests, 'Ritual defined in the most general and basic terms is a performance, planned or improvised, that effects a transition from everyday life to an alternative context within which the everyday is transformed ... Traditional religious rituals open up ordinary life to ultimate reality or some transcendent being or force in order to tap its transformative power' (1997: 139).[1] Alexander's definition of religious ritual could well be applied to Woody Allen's *The Purple Rose of Cairo*, with its notion of two worlds ('everyday life' and an 'alternative context'), alongside the opening up to something other and transformative.

By now I hope it is apparent what such a definition of ritual might contribute to the view of the worldmaking and re-creative dimensions of cinema and religion for which I am arguing. The altar and the screen offer an alternative to the everyday world, and there are semi-permeable passages between the two worlds so that everyday life is transformed. In other words, there are openings from one to the other and it becomes necessary to know how to access these openings. In *The Matrix*, the characters had to be transported through particular telephonic 'landlines'; access from one world to the other was, curiously, hardwired and cell phones did not allow access. Similarly, rituals, if done correctly at the right time and place, provide passports between worlds, and the transformation operates via performative structures. Among other things, in performances actors dress up, clothing themselves in seemingly authentic costumes, contributing to the world re-creative activities of the dramatic enactment. Such 'clothing', to harken back to Clifford Geertz's metaphorical terminology of clothing in his definition of religion, enables the creation of an 'aura of factuality' that seems 'uniquely realistic' (1973: 90). Both dramas and rituals rely on such clothing, bringing the alternative world into the here and now, not simply 'representing' but 're-presenting' that other world.

Other descriptions of ritualistic elements that are crucial here include: the emphasis on the patterned, and often rhythmic, performances of rituals; the ways they sometimes embody and act out myths; and the role they have in helping humans remember – we need rituals because, as Peter Berger tells it, 'men forget' (1967: 40).[2] Ultimately, worlds are constructed and re-created in and through space and time. Likewise, rituals *take place, in time*, helping to construct the larger worlds of which they are a part. Five times a day, in accordance with the sun's rising and setting, observant Muslims all over the world pray, and they do so facing the central shrine of Islam, the Kaba. Similarly, the space of Jewish synagogues around the world is oriented so that the ark, which houses the Torah scrolls and the direction for prayer, has the congregants facing Jerusalem, and ultimately the now-remains of the great Temple. In so doing, observers in both traditions perform rituals in their present space, at a particular time, and are linked to a larger community in the present, just as their spatial orientation links them to a historical continuity. These rituals are rhythmic, conducted according to a cosmic sense of time, and re-enact ancient myths and traditions from other places and times. By engaging with ritual in a present place, humans are connected with and remember the past. Space and time become fused in the ritual setting.

Films are created through similar spatial and temporal dimensions. Filmmakers work with and manipulate afilmic space, time, form, movement, colour and sound in ways that look and feel similar to how rituals are experienced through the use of sensual things like flowers, music, candles, symbols, cosmic relations and images, and in connection with the great myths of old. The world beyond is brought here to us, onscreen, as afilmic reality becomes profilmic reality, and just as time and space are shown to be malleable elements of the cosmos. And so again, by thinking about filmic structures we might learn about ritual structures and vice versa. Film viewing *can* itself become a ritual, or at least incorporated into rituals (see chapters 3 and 4), but they are not necessarily so.[3]

At the risk of oversimplification, space is re-created onscreen through the various components that make up 'the shot', especially cinematography and *mise-en-scène*. A shot of a man (and it typically is a man) from a low camera angle emphasises one thing about him, usually that he is important and has authority. A camera that tilts down in a shot can serve to create a connection between things above and things below, as already suggested. In a like manner, film theorist Robert Kolker discusses the physical space created in Buster Keaton films, suggesting, 'Only film can make things look "real" by means of fabricating and composing reality out of a trick occurring in space' (2002: 23). Further, 'Our response to Keaton's images is ... the response of our fantasy of what the world might have looked like. Even in Keaton, though, we do not see the world itself. We see its image. Its memory. And that remains strong enough, present enough to surprise and delight us' (ibid.). All camera movements and angles help create a world that transcends the technological apparatus, that points towards another world, to 'what the world might have looked like'. This is language uncannily similar to the language describing ritual above.

Space is re-created on film for narrative, mythical and ideological purposes, just as it (more simply) helps to create a character's identity and relationship with her/his world. What I am interested in here are the ways camera movements replicate or challenge existing cosmological structures, as we have already seen with *Blue Velvet* and *Star Wars*, and bring these structures down to earth, to an environment within which viewers can relate. The choice between tilting a camera up and down or setting up a horizontal tracking shot to create a scene is a choice that defines the space of the filmic image, including the relations between characters, each other and their environment. Likewise, rituals are also conducted within spaces, and those spaces are arranged along X and Y axes.

Again risking oversimplification, the essential element of time onscreen is created through the processes of editing, of taking individual shots and placing them next to other shots. A shot, as the great Soviet proponent of editing Sergei Eisenstein suggested, is 'a piece of an event' (1992a: 132), and the mixture of shots can create a 'potential energy', and that for Eisenstein was of central importance for filmmaking, re-creating the overall event. As the editor Paul Hirsch claims, 'Editing is very interesting and absorbing work because of the illusions you can create. You can span thirty years within an hour and a half. You can stretch a moment in slow motion. You can play with time in extraordinary ways' (1992: 188–9). The editing of shots creates the proverbial sum as larger than its parts. A world can be re-created through editing, magical things can happen (things appear and disappear) and eons can be transversed in seconds.

Contemporary Hollywood films have been estimated to average around 800–1,200 shots in a ninety-minute feature presentation, which means that a single shot does not stay onscreen for more than five seconds, on average.[4] When reviewers discuss films as 'fast-paced', they are referring not just to movement onscreen, but primarily to the effects of rapid editing. On one level, such speed marks a contrast with traditional religious iconography whereby religious adherents sit in front of a 'static' image for lengthy periods of time in order to receive the *baraka/darshan*/blessings of the gods and goddesses. Films create worlds, and religious adherents are altered by their experiences of cinema. That contemporary US films include so many cuts – much more than earlier films or even most films from other parts of the world – begins to suggest something of the relation between 'speed' and the constructs of a culture that sees itself as 'fast-paced'.

In the end, rituals and films both operate in and through the worldly dimensions of space and time, morphing and massaging, re-creating and re-establishing an alternative world out there and bringing it into the here and now.

II. Spatialising worlds and cinematography

Most writers have a certain set of stock narrative structures from which to create a screenplay – whether they are conscious of it or whether these stories somehow archetypically remain in the unconscious is not my interest here. The hero journey is a prominent template for screenplays (for example, *Gladiator, Braveheart, Shrek*) as are rites of passage stories including coming of age tales (*The Sandlot, Dangerous Lives of Altar Boys, The Lion King*), weddings (*Four Weddings and a Funeral, The Wedding Planner*) and funerals (*The Funeral, The Big Chill, Last Orders*). Other rituals like pilgrimages are habitually retold for the cinema (*The Wizard of Oz, The Blues Brothers, The Straight Story*).

Often mixed with these traditional rituals are other narratives about the merging of two worlds. William Paden suggests, 'Religions create, maintain and oppose worlds' (1994: 53), and the opposition of two or more created worlds becomes a great narrative device. *Monsoon Wedding* (2002) and *My Big, Fat, Greek Wedding* (2002) are both about the rite of passage that is a wedding, but through the ceremony two different worlds are brought, indeed forced, together: Hindu parents who practise arranged marriages are mixed with a younger generation who are uneasy about the arrangements; Protestant and Greek Orthodox families must get along for the sake of their relatives' love interests.

Other films such as *Nuovo cinema Paradiso* (*Cinema Paradiso*, 1988) explicitly rely on the creation of dual sacred spaces – in this case, the theatre and the church – to create their conflict. Giuseppe Tornatore carefully sets up the two worlds within the first few minutes, displaying the impoverishment of the church ritual (in which altar boys regularly fall asleep) opposed to the dynamism of the movie theatre (in which a deep sense of ritualised community occurs through its shared laughter and tears). In each of the spatial worlds portrayed in *Cinema Paradiso*, light is underscored within the spaces. The church is introduced through a narrow sun ray coming through a small window high up, barely able to illuminate the liturgical spaces below. Meanwhile the theatre projector's light pours through a lion's mouth, a mouth that, in the visionary eyes of the young Toto (Salvatore Cascio), roars a powerful roar. There is little question which lit space, and ultimately which ritualised world, is the most significant for the life of the community.

Similarly, Lasse Hallström's *Chocolat* (2000) sets up two contrasting spaces, and through these spaces, contrasting worlds. The establishing shot of the film begins outside a quaint French village set on a hill, and it is obvious that the church is at the centre of the town and at its highest point, dominating the other buildings. The first shots inside the church are either low angle or high angle, depending on whether the point of view is from the congregation or the pulpit, and a dramatic verticality is emphasised. This space is contrasted with the chocolate shop, just around the corner from the church. The pagan protagonist, Vianne (Juliette Binoche), comes to town, as the narrator puts it, as 'a sly wind blew in from the north', and sets up a chocolate shop, just in time for the Lenten season when the good Christians of the town are getting ready to abstain. Her small shop is shown as an inviting place, especially for those who have been rejected from other parts of society. Through straight-on, medium shots, Vianne is depicted behind the counter as if tending bar, while townspeople sit on stools and sample her sweets. These rituals are both profane and profound. Camera angles emphasise the horizontal nature of the chocolate shop, which is pitted against the church and especially the Comte Reynaud (Alfred Molina) who sternly runs the town both politically and religiously. A significant early shot is taken from the opening of what will become the chocolate shop, and the wide angle camera is forced to point high to take in the height of the church towering above it. In the

An early shot in *Chocolat* looks out from the soon-to-be chocolate shop onto the imposing church towering above

The Comte, standing as an 'upright' figure throughout *Chocolat*, eventually gives in to his desires and is found in a far from upright position in the chocolate shop

end, the Comte is transformed when he breaks into the chocolate shop and gives in to his desires, gorging on the sweets until he falls asleep. He is found by the priest, the next morning, sleeping in a horizontal position in the front window of the chocolate shop, in the shadow of the towering church. In the end, the two worlds become more or less reconciled as Vianne experiences a transformation of her own.

Antonia's Line

Few films set up two distinct worlds through their spatial orientation like Marleen Gorris's *Antonia's Line*. Similar to *Chocolat*, Gorris's film also contrasts a vertically-orientated world with a horizontally-orientated world: the first being re-presented through a traditional Christian, male-dominated church, while the other world is re-presented from the point of view of powerful but outsider female characters. Antonia's community is established in the courtyard of her farm, and this space is contrasted with a few others, most significantly that of the church. Both of these films structurally compare two communities, two forms of power wielded within the communities and the difference that gender makes in understanding the sacred.

Antonia's Line, winner of the Academy Award for Best Foreign Language Film in 1996, tells the story of Antonia (Willeke van Ammelrooy) and her 'lineage': her daughter Danielle (Els Dottermans), granddaughter (played by several actors including Veerle van Overloop) and great-granddaughter Sarah (Thyrza Ravesteijn). Bookended by her own dying day, the film moves back in time to introduce the creation of Antonia's family in a small town in Denmark and the community that forms around them.

In the beginning, Antonia returns to the land of her ancestors along with her daughter Danielle, not long after World War Two has ended. They come back to pay their last respects to Antonia's dying mother, a slightly crazed, pious woman. (Why Antonia left the place we never find out. Her departure was possibly due to the war, although when we meet the mother on her deathbed, we get a good suggestion it might have been for familial reasons.) As Antonia and Danielle step off the bus, they are framed by the camera below a sign that reads 'Welcome to our Liberators', a greeting intended for the British, American and Russian forces at the end of the war, but which takes on a secondary connotation when these two strong women walk beneath it. Indeed, through the course of the film, they 'liberate' many people along the way. Nonetheless, Antonia is not a separatist and does not rely on setting up her own oppositional space and rituals, but is instead able to move among the various important spaces of her town and of the film. For her mother's funeral, as throughout the film, Antonia attends church services, not because she believes any of it, but because she seems to feel it a duty. And at a few points she visits the male-dominated pub at various times of the week. Her ability to move between, and remain strong within, the various spaces demonstrates her ability to transcend gender-defined spaces.

Even so, the courtyard of her farm becomes the prominent site where the ritual functions of community take place. Sunday mornings are set in the church, and high and low camera angles take precedence, replicating the hierarchical authority structures set within the church. It is a male-dominated world, and verticality reigns. Sunday afternoons are spent in Antonia's courtyard, where an ever-increasing community of people are welcomed to sup at the great outdoor table. In these shots, the community is generally viewed through medium shots, at the level of the seated sup-plicants. Antonia, while ostensibly the 'head' of this creedless community, does not sit at the head of the table. Instead, all persons are gathered at the same level, just as the camera shoots them on a horizontal plane. Interestingly, one of the only times we see a high-angle shot in this environment is when the great granddaughter, Sarah, is sitting up high in the barn, looking down on the activities of the courtyard. Late in the film we learn that Sarah is actually the narrator of the whole story of 'Antonia's line', and her 'looking down' on the characters reveals something about the imaginative storytelling aspects. Up there, Sarah is able to imagine all the souls who have died through the generations, dancing together in the courtyard; in other words, in the space of the courtyard, even verticality is transposed into a creative, collective community that transcends time to gather all together.

Ritual studies scholar Lesley Northrup has written astutely about the gendered differences that verticality and horizontality make in ritualised settings. Northrup critiques some of the dominant modes of understanding ritual, especially that given by comparative religions scholar Mircea Eliade and his followers, who emphasise the vertical dimension of the sacred, the notion that there is a 'hierophany' in which the divine 'comes down' to the earth, creating an *axis mundi*, a central axis connecting the earth to the heavens. (The film production company logos, discussed in the introduction, could be seen as a type of *axis mundi*.) For Islam it is the stone shrine, the Kaba in Mecca, that serves this function. For ancient Israel, and many in contemporary Judaism, it is the Holy of Holies at the centre of the Temple in Jerusalem. In any case, it is a vertical shaft originating in the heavens (always 'above') into the earth below. Such cosmological comprehensions are reaffirmed in sacred architecture, and this building is ultimately replicated in cinematographic constructions of the sacred. Northrup suggests, 'Sacred space, far from being simply an adjunct liturgical consideration, is a core datum in women's ritual experience' (1997: 58). And while we 'moderns' know there is no up or down in space, films take much from the pre-eminence of the vertical, establishing powerful characters through points of view that emphasise height; it is little secret that such characters are usually male.

Significantly, and I would argue more importantly, Antonia's courtyard stands not only in opposition to the church, but also to the Schopenhauer-inspired, atheistic outlook on the world given by Antonia's dear friend Crooked Finger (Mil Seghers). Having survived the miserable war, Crooked Finger refuses to bathe or leave his book-bedecked cave of a home. And

In *Antonia's Line*, Crooked Finger dies alone, in a dramatically vertical position...

...while in contrast, Antonia dies horizontally, surrounded by friends and family

while the same fate – namely death – awaits everyone, the spatiality of Crooked Finger's death in comparison to Antonia tells a great deal about the worlds in which they live. A brief shot of the dead body of Crooked Finger, hanging from the rafters in his home after he kills himself, emphasises a dramatic verticality. His body is elongated, pointing like a pencil from floor to roof, as he dies alone. In contrast, Antonia's death, like her friend Lara's before her, occurs in the horizontal space of the bedroom, surrounded by her family and friends. Even in death (especially there) a supine, horizontal orientation creates an invitation to community, bring-ing people together ritualistically, while the vertical precludes others.

Antonia's Line and *Chocolat* both present sexual differences through spatial means. There are men's worlds, hierarchically/vertically ordered, and there are women's worlds, egalitarian/horizontally ordered. In cre-ating such spatial worlds, these films re-present the possibility of re-created ritual activity through new orientations. These films (and here I would include *Cinema Paradiso*) are all, on the surface, anti-religious. The Christian church in each comes off looking a bit silly, sad and inca-pable of relating to the alternative realities created in the movie theatre, chocolate shop and courtyard, in the respective films. But if one frees oneself from looking only at the representation of religion *in* film, and looks at broader structures of worldmaking with regard to rituals, it is easy to see how each of these films offers an alternative world that is itself *deeply religious*. The 'female spaces' of these films are generally accepting and affirming (except to rapists and spouse-abusers) and offer a different sense of community to the hierarchy from above. There is no escape from responsibility in this orientation, but the responsibility is recast so as to connect with those in the immediate community, not because of an authority on high.

III. Editing the everyday: producing the sacred

Ritualising occurs in space, but also in time, and religious worlds are con-stituted through spatial and temporal dimensions. Likewise, filmmakers capture afilmic space and time for the purposes of presenting a world onscreen. Turning now to the time elements, the following section seeks to display the ways time is re-created through the vital activity of editing.

Editing connects. Editing reconnects. Editing even goes so far as to connect totally unconnected fragments of space and time with other frag-ments of space and time. That is the truth of the technical enterprise. Editing takes one framed image (including actors, costumes, lighting and so forth) and connects it with another image, even if that image is out of synch, out of time, out of country, with the previous shot. Editing, from the view of some theorists and filmmakers, can create conflict, putting the viewer on the edge of their seat, intellectually reassembling what is presented.

In the following section we shall explore the ways everyday life, or 'the profane', is filmed and then edited in ways that juxtapose one person/ place/thing with another, thereby creating something larger and more powerful than its parts. The profane literally means 'outside the temple' (from the Latin *pro-fanus*). It is ordinary life and time. There is nothing inherently wrong or bad about it, but it is not to be confused with the 'sacred' (that which is 'set apart', holds power). After a re-view of *Cinema Paradiso*, two films that work with a series of profane images will be examined, to show how through their juxtapositions, their explosive montages, a sacred world is produced. Segments of these films, separated by seven decades, that speak to the rhythms, repetitions and re-creations of ritualised life will be explored.

Beyond the spatial contrasts, *Cinema Paradiso* also explicitly references the role of editing in ways deeply resonant with a religious studies understanding of the *sacred*. The sacred are those objects, persons, times, places, texts, that are 'set apart' from everyday life. Sacred things contain power that fascinates just as it remains mysterious, can bless or curse, function as an orientation point for religious worlds. Father Adelfio (Leopoldo Trieste) presides over both church and theatres, and watches a private first showing of all films screened at the Cinema Paradiso, censoring any violence or public displays of affection between the actors. Alfredo (Philippe Noiret) the projectionist dutifully cuts out the scenes from the celluloid film and while he is supposed to splice them back in before he sends the reels back, he often forgets. The result is a projection booth filled with sections of film, which fascinates the young Toto. Over time Toto steals some of the strips and keeps them in a box under his bed, along with a picture of his father who he gradually learns was killed in the war. In a night-time scene, reminiscent of a child's bedtime prayers, Toto takes out the images and looks at them, re-enacting the scenarios from the frames. Later when Toto's family's home burns, we learn that it was these highly-flammable celluloid strips that caused the fire. And at the end of the film, a grown-up Toto (Jacques Perrin) sits watching a film by himself in a small screening theatre. Alfredo, who became something of a surrogate father to Toto, edited the film before he died. It is made up of all the kisses, all the near-nude images, all the passion that was denied to the film viewers of the Cinema Paradiso. The now-successful filmmaker Toto sits weeping as he watches kiss after kiss, cathartically celebrating passion at the same time as he mourns the death of his friend. There are fewer representations of the sacred onscreen better than the censored film strips that function through *Cinema Paradiso*. They are set apart, placed in a box under a bed and left hanging on walls; meanwhile they contain the potential to kill and to inspire, to retain memories and to orientate life.

Man with a Movie Camera and Baraka

At the height of the Soviet experiments with montage – Sergei Eisenstein, Vsevolod Pudovkin, Lev Kuleshov and others – Dziga Vertov gives us a day in the urban socialist life. Workers are productive, happy, have time for play, sport and recreation. But when a man with a movie camera, for example, investigates the times and spaces outside of the temple, trans-formations take place. The camera/cameraman duo become priestly, sha-manistic, taking in the sights, sounds, spaces and temporal unfoldings of the world and representing them in new ways.

While the film appears to be centred on a single city in a single day, it was actually filmed across several Russian cities, taking many days to shoot. The film viewers experience a collapsing of space and time, just as they are invited to participate in this remade world: the opening and clos-ing frames present the entire film as a presentation that can only occur in the film theatre. Self-referentially, the film notes its own worldmaking capa-bilities through editing as a horse-drawn carriage moving down a street suddenly halts and the film cuts to an editing room and we find editors peering at strips of film, attempting to assemble a whole out of the imaged parts. All of a sudden a horse stops in its tracks, a girl's smile is extended throughout time, the profane activities of life are halted, examined, scru-tinised, praised and then spliced back into the ongoing machinations of urbanity. Through looking at the otherwise overlooked, the movement of a horse or the facial expression of a child is highlighted and brought to a grander life through the activities of a man with a movie camera.

Man with a Movie Camera shows that history is made up of the small events, the everyday, and includes births, deaths, marriages, even divorces. This is cinema not simply as 'reality', but more importantly as 'truth' (*kino-pravda*, as Vertov called it, 'cinematic truth') in which the camera operator simply goes out into the streets and *captures* what is there to be seen. And yet, by focusing on the profane, the everyday and taking the events to the editing room, the film gives insight into the extraordinary events of life: birth, death, love, community. In a day's time, in a single city, we see the range of life, the miraculous, and it is only through the world's re-creation that the sacredness of such profane activities can occur.

Similarly, Ron Fricke, the director of the experimental film *Baraka*, somewhat vaguely suggests that the film is 'a journey of rediscovery that plunges into nature, into history, into the human spirit, and finally into the realm of the infinite'.[5] The film was shot with a large format 70mm camera, offering precise definition of many remote places, and was filmed in 24 different countries around the world. Containing no words, with no main characters or even a guiding narrator, the film nonetheless tells a story audio-visually. It is arguable whether it is the audio (stunning music, synchronised from instruments around the world) or the visual (stunning images, synchronised from shots around the world) that plays the key role here. What is true is that they blend almost seamlessly through the editing process to produce a vision of the world that draws connections between places, times and traditions.

Baraka is a Sufi word meaning 'blessing', also etymologically related to 'breath', and as we watch and think and listen, we realise the direct relations between blessing and breathing. There are precious few religious traditions that do not take breath as an atomic component to their worlds. The human body needs breath, constantly, without fail. *Baraka* shows us a world of tactility, of visuality, of scents and aural impulses. It provides a window onto the lived, felt experiences of religion and culture.

Baraka begins its presentation with the same kinds of images that constitute the production credits of many films: lofty heights, clouds, mountaintops and lunar landscapes. Fricke shows these images in the first few shots, introducing viewers to the cosmic order of things leaving out the human countenance for some time. The first couple of shots of the film display the Himalayas, the grandest elevations in non-aviated human history, conjuring with them thoughts of some of the longest lasting religious traditions in human history, the mythologies of what has come to be known as the Hindu tradition. The *Mahabharata* tells us, 'At the time of creation, the Grandfather, full of fiery energy, created living beings.' Some time later the reader of the *Mahabharata* learns that this creation is set in the Himalayas, and is the home of Shiva. We are thus connected up within a creation myth.

In a like manner, the third shot tilts up a mountain, which is placed before a fourth shot tilting down a totally different mountain, now thousands of miles away in Japan, focusing on a Japanese snow monkey seemingly settled in high-altitude hot springs. Myth sutures geographies and becomes connected to the animated lives of animals. Here it is difficult not to read an alternative cosmology into the film, this time an evolutionary theme. The hunch is reaffirmed a few minutes later through shots of the famous Galapagos Iguanas, creatures on the islands that inspired Charles Darwin's work stemming from his early 'Voyage of the Beagle' (1839). *Baraka* includes all of this: creation myths from around the world and scientific myths about the world's origins.

As with *Man With a Movie Camera*, *Baraka* is structured from the sun shining in the morning to eventual sunset, showing a 'day in the life'. For Fricke, that day is a day of the world, not just Bolshevik Russia, and that world's day is also something of a *yuga* in the Hindu sense, an epoch/age that begins and ends, only to allow a new age to start anew. Startling juxtapositions in the film include an image of a stack of human femurs cutting to a stack of military artillery, Scottish bagpipes mixed with Japanese *Koto* drums as images of burning oil refineries in southern Iraq are displayed.

Most of the film provides a view of the various worlds in which humans live. The viewer generally is positioned as a spectator, to overlook the conditions of, variously, urbanisation, religious rituals, military build-up, the aftermath of genocide, the moon and stars in rotation, mass transport or animals in the service of humans, to name but a few. Critically, the film does not completely allow a distanced viewing. Instead, through the rhythmic use of sound (wind instruments, mechanised breathing noises), coupled with rhythmic editing, the viewer gains a certain perceived intimacy with the world. As the images unfold, one can begin to imagine the interconnectedness of all things. This may be a fiction and a false sense of enlightenment, but also demonstrates the power in manipulations of space and time.

Ron Fricke makes his worldly point a bit more subtly than Godfrey Reggio, with whom he worked as cinematographer and editor on Reggio's *Koyaanisqatsi* (from the Hopi, 'life out of balance'). *Koyaanisqatsi* showed the mixture of everyday life with global politics, sped up and slowed down, edited together and mixed with Philip Glass's minimalist score. But Fricke succeeds in places where Reggio tries to make too fine a point. *Baraka* displays a fundamental ambiguity between the cyclical view of a world heading into a spiral that may continue on into another world, and a world spinning out of control. In the end, its never clear whether the film has an apocalyptic message: the end of the world as 'we' (civilised humans) know it, or just part of an ongoing cycle of decay, death and rebirth, with the whole thing starting over again at 'the end'. The final scenes of *Baraka* are of a diminished sun, the end of a day.

To conclude this section, I offer a comparison of a scene in *Man with a Movie Camera* and *Baraka*, where I believe Fricke might have been making a direct reference to Vertov: the scene of the cigarette factory woman. Vertov's socialist vision of the worker depicts a smiling young woman who later is shown leaving the factory and possibly going out for an evening of socialising. Vertov's vision is of the worker as sacralised, lifted beyond her

Contributing to the good of the society: Vertov's cigarette factory worker performs her repetitive labour with a smile on her face

Bound to a faceless global capitalism: Fricke's cigarette factory worker performs her repetitive labour in the midst of hundreds of other workers

profane life to interact with something more transcendent. This transcenduent is not a god, nor found in a religious space, but rather it is the life of the worker, acting for the good of the society as a whole that creates the transcendent in the 1920s Soviet world.

Fricke's worker is found in Southeast Asia, six decades of modernisation and globalisation later. The mundane, repetitive task of filling papers with tobacco, trimming the ends of the cigarettes and stacking them, alongside a warehouse full of other women doing the same chore, is shown only for a minute or so in real time, but that is plenty enough to drive home the point that there is no local community for which one's work is any longer meaningful. There is only global consumption as the viewer is connected to this larger world when, soon after the cigarette factory is depicted, the film cuts to a man standing at a Tokyo subway stop smoking a cigarette, seemingly unaware of all the life that surrounds him.

The world created in *Baraka* is one so vast it rarely speaks to a personal life within it – though it does do that significantly, from time to time – yet relies on universal prescriptions of the sacred. For Vertov's communist and/ or socialist ideal, the world is small enough to still maintain a direct relation between the work of the individual and the larger society. For Fricke's globalised, over-industrialised world, work is a profane activity that cannot reach transcendent significance for the individual.

Conclusion

There is an emphasis on myths and rituals through this book for two reasons. Firstly, they have had profound power over individuals and communities for millennia and the contemporary age is no exception, in spite of certain liberal, rationalist strains that have attempted to eradicate them. You can exorcise 'God' from society, and even from religion, but myths and rituals are lasting human endeavours because they function at levels of worldmaking, and it is not possible (at least sanely) to go without worlds. Further, they are interconnected: myths need rituals to survive, to live on into ever new permutations, while ritual needs myth for its rootedness in the creations of worlds. The next two chapters will show the ways film meets its viewers directly, offering new forms of ritualising.

In the end, just what does watching camera movements teach us about religion? At least this: the student of religion can learn about the ups and downs and side to side movements of rituals, and ask what difference it makes. An awareness of space, in two or more dimensions, can challenge us to rethink the spaces in which religions take place. Is verticality simply a matter of up and down (sometimes, to paraphrase Freud, a cigar *is* just a cigar), or does it serve to construct a world of hierarchical power? Likewise, can rituals become more egalitarian through operating on a more horizontal plane? There are no blanket answers here, and a strict dichotomy between vertical and horizontal is not helpful. Nonetheless, spatial dimensions can often be ideologically charged, displaying gender roles and more general identities within worlds.

Film editing, through its juxtapositions of varying times and spaces, highlights connections across the world in ways unintelligible to the unaided eye. Time is malleable, and the seemingly chaotic movements of a place like New York's Grand Central Station, depicted in *Baraka*, can be sped up through time-lapse photography to reveal a strangely satisfying order. Chaos seems to hide in the cosmos and vice versa. To see anew, the camera and the editing booth provide alternative perspectives on the ebbs and flows of the world.

Filmmaking has long relied on the elements of ritual, whether filmmakers know this or not. Space and time, flowers and candles and sensual objects all make up the alternative worlds at the altars of the world's religions. Editors and cinematographers reproduce and ultimately re-create the lights and sights of rituals and put them onscreen, inviting viewers to take a step across that boundary. The two worlds are attached, interconnected, and each impinges on and impedes and enlivens the other. We are destitute without the interaction.

3   RELIGIOUS CINEMATICS: THE IMMEDIATE BODY
IN THE MEDIA OF FILM

The creation myth of cinema goes something like this: in a Paris café in December 1895, Auguste and Louis Lumière projected several films onto a wall. A bemused audience had gathered to see the latest in a string of imagistic inventions that emerged throughout the nineteenth century – from the reconceived *camera obscura* to the newer *camera lucida* and stereoscopes, from the daguerreotype to photographic film and eventually colour photographs – all offering fascinating new modes for re-seeing the world. The viewers that winter night were apparently not disappointed. The films were all silent, single-reel, lasting less than a minute, portraying everyday events of modern urban life such as workers leaving a factory, the demolition of a wall and, most famously, a train arriving at a station. The latter was shot with the film camera mounted on a train platform, as if the cinematographer-turned-viewer was waiting for the train her/his self and the action unfolds as the train moves towards the camera. In popular retellings of the initial viewing, some of the Parisians watching *L'Arrivée d'un train à la Ciotat* (*The Arrival of a Train at la Ciotat*, 1895) that evening jumped from their chairs and even began to run away as the train seemingly came through the walls of the café. With this screening, and a popular retelling of the event of that screening, we are firmly in the realm of myth.

A number of scholars have attempted to demythologise these origins of cinema, particularly when the retelling smacks of a pedantic, contemporary viewpoint looking back on 'those' naïve viewers in the beginning.[1] Whether or not viewers in that café actually got up from their chairs may never be known for sure, but one does not need to go any further than the local multi-plex to observe the ways in which the audio-visual experience of film works on the body: audiences sit engrossed in the unfolding scenes onscreen, jumping back in their chairs at suspenseful moments, weeping at poignant scenarios acted out, hiding their eyes at the scary parts. There is a visceral reaction to film. To go a step further towards proving the extreme bodily responses possible among the *fin-de-siècle* Parisians, one merely needs to attend a contemporary screening of a 3-D film: here audiences actively reach out to grasp objects and creatures that seem to come off the screen and into the theatre space. Significant improvements to 3-D films occurred throughout the latter half of the twentieth century, and their continued technological development in the early twenty-first century appears to be one of the more exciting futures for cinema. In each of these developments one thing remains constant: the perceiving body in the screening space is an active body, perpetually in motion.

In the beginning, then, what I am terming 'religious cinematics' is con-cerned with *the body in motion*. This chapter takes up the issue not just of the 'moving picture', but also of the 'moving body' and of the relations between the two. The relation between filmic and bodily movement, I sug-gest, has much to do with traditional religious ritual, especially when par-ticular film images strike the bodily senses and cause the body to move in response to an aesthetic, formalised liturgy of represented words, images and sounds. By not simply focusing on some religious *content* of a film but on the bodily responses to it, I attempt to take seriously the formal struc-tures of film and the ways it works sensually and aesthetically and how this is part and parcel of the ways traditional religious rituals have operated.

The first section below will introduce some of the theoretical, critical dimensions of a religious cinematics. The investigation here takes place within a long-standing philosophical and cognitive investigation into the relation between haptics and optics, the point at which *vision is felt*; between the ways in which film is never 'merely' image and/or sound but always multi-medial, impacting the various senses of the human body and causing it to shudder or sob, laugh or leap.[2] What I aim to outline (or at least point towards, since my ultimate trajectory shoots beyond or before rational language) is a movement of the body that is pre-conscious, before rational awareness, of Maruice Merleau-Ponty's 'aesthesio-' before the '-logical' body. Thus, in the final two sections I argue for the importance of avant-garde film, since that seems to be a privileged location for filmic experience that takes seriously the relation of aesthetics and logic. What is opened up via such films is an encounter with the 'face of the other', to use the language of the religio-ethical philosopher Emmanuel Levinas. On film, the face becomes something supremely real, deeply encountered by viewers, and confronted with this countenance the viewer cannot maintain their own stability. Finally, via Stan Brakhage's 'unwatchable' film, *The Act of Seeing With One's Own Eyes*, I make the case for moments of 'cinematic mysticism', when the categorising functions of film and the senses break down. In sensual confrontation with the filmic image of the dead body, I suggest that a religious cinematics has a powerful potential to escape its mediated confines and bring a viewing body face to face with death. As such, images and bodies merge in an experience not unlike that of the mystical experience, when borders, divisions and media all break down. In this way, a renewing function of filmic ritual emerges.

I. Religious cinematics: from film to body and back

> The artist has carried the tradition of vision and visualisation down through the ages. In the present time a very few have continued the process of visual perception in its deepest sense and transformed their inspirations into cinematic experiences. They create a new language made possible by the moving picture image. They create where fear before them has created the greatest necessity. They are essentially preoccupied by and deal imagistically with birth, sex, death and the search for God. (Brakhage 1978: 120)

About the making of his avant-garde film *Wavelength* (1967), Michael Snow stated: 'I wanted to make a summation of my nervous system, religious inklings and aesthetic ideas' (in Sitney 2002: 352). In response to such a statement one might immediately raise the question: what possible 'religious inkling' could be expressed in a film that for 45 minutes does little more than slowly zoom in on a small picture from across an almost empty room? What does the nervous system have to do with it? To put it more generally, what is the nature of the relationship between the formal and structural components of avant-garde filmmaking and religious experience? I cannot be sure if what I have to say in the following resembles the intents of Snow or Brakhage, but it provides an answer for the relation of religion and the corporeal, nervous activity of seeing.

Like the scientific investigations of its variant spelling 'kinematics', and more specifically with that of its etymological cousin 'kinetics' (according to the *Oxford English Dictionary*, 'The branch of dynamics which investigates the relations between the motions of bodies and the forces acting upon them') religious cinematics is concerned with the motion of the human body being acted upon by the audio-visual forces of film. My aim here is to look at the relation *between* motion pictures and moving bodies and some of the particular ways in which films can stir the body to action. Ultimately, I consider, there is a deep resonance to religious ritual found within this interaction; yet, to understand it, we must first break down the relation and analyse the various media that exist between image and body.

By 'media' I do not merely mean what too often goes by that name: high-tech, electronic media such as the Internet, television or even, more broadly, 'mass media'. Rather, I intend it in its more literal and primal form as something 'in the middle'. Being 'in the middle' of things, *in media res*, is to alter the relations between the things themselves, so that media end up working as a 'filter', by which substances are sorted, categorised and thus forced to become something other than they were 'originally'. (Without getting too far into metaphysical speculation here, it is indeed questionable to say there is any *thing* in an original form; rather things only exist as they are embodied, mediated, put into form.) To say, with Marshall McLuhan (1964), that 'the medium is the message', may be slightly hyperbolic, but not by much.

In terms of religious cinematics, singular film images do not simply meet a singular body mass. Rather, images are sifted and sorted, compartmentalised and catalogued, as they are taken in by the seeing body. Herein I am dealing with two varieties of media. The first is the medium of film, whereby the sounds and images of the world outside are filtered through the various apparatus of film production. These mediated sounds and images are then engaged by the second medium, the bodily sense receptors; most specifically those dealing with hearing and seeing, even as an all-important synaesthetic response occurs so that the body is ultimately *touched* and stirred to movement. Just as filmic sounds and images are understood to be mediated, so, my argument goes, should bodily perceptions of these sounds and images be understood as having a mediating effect. The medium of sense perception is the corollary to the medium of film.

To reiterate, film images and the body must be understood in light of their *media*. Film, as the term is most broadly understood, is a medium, as are print, oral speech and oil painting. The filmic medium works through recording and projecting apparatuses. These technological mechanisms capture images from the world 'out there' which are then filtered through the processes of framing, shaping, bending, twisting, condensing and reshaping, and varied by differences in light, colour, frame size, film stock, computer editing programs and projector bulbs, among other mechanical influences. The result is a world that is re-created through the medium of film. We may recognise the train on the screen from our experiences in the world outside, but its structure, shape and power have been altered through its filmic appearance. This much is hardly news.

What is perhaps more challenging is the idea that the other side of the equation – that is, the body – is also part of a mediated system. To discuss this, I reappropriate 'aesthetics' here as the name for such a focus. Aesthetics, in its etymological guise, studies that which 'pertains to sense perception' (from the Greek, *aesthetikos*). I assert that *sense perception is the medium of the body*, and if we want to understand aesthetics (meaning everything from theories of art, to judgements on beauty, to cultural tastes) we have to start with the body and its senses. The human sense organs perform an analogous role to that of artistic and communications media. That is, they function as an intervening substance that alters the world 'as it is' (leaving aside metaphysical questions of the nature of reality). Sense perception binds the body, shapes it, controls its input and output. The sense organs are passageways between the inside and outside of the body, a connection between the internal and external worlds. Sounds and images affect the body through the bodily sense organs of the ears and eyes – connected ultimately to the cerebral cortex and all its compartmentalising functions – and it is ultimately this sensual, *mediating*, experience that causes the body in the theatre (or wherever) to move.

The human senses are trained from infancy to categorise the sights, sounds and smells of the world by cultural and technological forces. How we see, how we touch and how we taste are all part of the social construction of reality. But where sociologists like Peter Berger tend to stress the role of language in this process, I am pointing towards a more primary locus (which is not to say it is the origin) for worldmaking: the senses of the human body. For in learning what smells and sights to privilege and which to shun, we construct our worlds. Social worldmaking, like the mythical creation of the world in Judeo-Christian contexts, is never 'out of nothing', but always a matter of separation, selection and focus. (Compare God's creative activity in Genesis 1: there is the creative work that comes from speech, but there is the second and equally important activity of separation: light from dark, land from sea, and ultimately the first human is literally split in two as God creates the two sexes out of one.)[3] From the sense experiences that we take in from the world around us we select particular sounds and feelings, arrange them in the reflective capacities of our mind and forget all that does not pertain to us. This creates and maintains the world in a familiar way and allows us to get along in social environments.

Over the course of human development, what emerges is what Maurice Merleau-Ponty calls the aesthesiological body, an entity in which sensation and rational thought work together and sometimes against each other. Merleau-Ponty did more than any other modern philosopher to bring philosophy 'back to its senses' and to argue for a sensual mode of thinking. The aesthesiological body is in distinction to the rationalised senses – particularly the eye, as epitomised by René Descartes – in which vision operates from a single-point perspective, observing the world from a stable point of view and calculating its components. Merleau-Ponty suggests that Descartes, while attempting to be phenomenological, did not go far enough with his descriptions. Without motion, the eye sees a *measurable* thing. The observing subject is provided a knowledge that exists in and through pure motionlessness (two-dimensional), and it is certain of this. This, according to Merleau-Ponty, was Descartes' visual mistake, and he counters the stillness of certainty when he states 'vision is attached to movement' (1993: 124). This statement may seem innocuous in itself, but the eye that sees is an eye in motion, bound, as it is, with the body. Vision is not something which resides in the mind, or the *cogito*, or the *ego*, a place of final assurance and knowledge that something is there. Rather, vision resides within the body. With the body we must confront the enigma of 'overlapping': 'the fact that my body simultaneously sees and is seen' (ibid.). (And from such an idea, Jacques Lacan (1978) formulated his thoughts on the look and the gaze, so important for later film studies, though Lacan's structure was always more visually isolated and had little impact on the relations of the seeing body.) The 'self' implied here is not the assimilating self which is assured of its beliefs, but 'a self by confusion … a self, then, that is caught up in things' (Merleau-Ponty 1993: 124). The whole and certain self which says 'I' and sees clearly must be abandoned for an eye which is *in medias res*. 'I live it from the inside; I am immersed in it' (1993: 138). 'The visible about us seems to rest in itself. It is as though our vision were formed in the heart of the visible, or as though there were between it and us an intimacy as close as between the sea and the strand' (Merleau-Ponty 1967: 130–1). Though Merleau-Ponty spent little time writing about the cinema, his notions here have much to do with the interrelation of filmic image and sensing body.

The aesthesiological body, according to Merleau-Ponty, resides at the intertwining – the in-between, mediating space – of the invisible and the visible: 'My body as a visible thing is contained within the full spectacle. But my seeing body subtends this visible body and all the visibles within it. There is reciprocal insertion and intertwining of one in the other' (1967: 138). The body can both see and is seen; because of this it is subject to the impulses of the world, including film images. The aesthesiological body brings together ideas and the sensible world; knowledge of ideas does not come about through an abstracted, bodiless mind. Rather, 'however we finally have to understand it, the "pure" ideality already streams forth along the articulations of the aesthesiological body' (1993: 152). Thoughts and feelings work together in the worldmaking enterprise.

Because ideas are never separate from the bodies that help produce them, one of the more intriguing dimensions to Merleau-Ponty's quasi-empiricist articulation here is a certain affirmation of *doubt* within epistemological language. His writings on vision work against the rationalism, the certainty and the measured perspectives of a great deal of philosophy. Merleau-Ponty makes a strong argument for the doubting, empirical subject. This is a sensing subject who remains open to the world and therefore willing to move and be moved. Likewise, the aesthesiological body becomes key to my analysis of religious cinematics.[4]

It is doubt that stirs up the twitching, tearful, tense body that moves in front of the two-dimensions of the motion picture. And it is doubt that opens the doors for the believing body to experience a larger world. Adult humans are made up from a complex body that contains aesthetic and rational experiences, among other configurations, and the very complexity of this intertwining demonstrates paradoxes and desires. For psychoana-lytic film theorist Christian Metz, following the work of Freud and Lacan, the subjectivity of the film viewer is ultimately split, simultaneously con-taining multiple perspectives and viewpoints: 'I shall say that behind any [filmic] fiction there is a second fiction: the diegetic events are fictional, that is the first; but everyone pretends to believe that they are true, and that is the second; there is even a third: the general refusal to admit that *somewhere in oneself* one believes they are genuinely true' (1977: 72; emphasis added). Metz's analysis here could just as well be applied to the function of religious myth: performers of traditional rituals often ration-ally know the ancient story they are re-enacting in their rites is fictional; meanwhile somewhere within the self is the tinge of recognition that the story might in fact be true and the ritualising bodies act as if it were so. Moreover, and here I am extrapolating on Merleau-Ponty's and Metz's thoughts, these layers of fiction have to do with the corporeal-aesthetic experience in contrast to the reasoning, reflective, cognitive dimensions of mind. What I want to suggest in the brief space of this chapter is that this 'somewhere in oneself' is the space of the body in motion: that moving entity that escapes the rational mind, that stirring of the leg muscles that makes us want to run from the projected images; that corporeal impulse to bow down before a deity that we know is not somehow 'above' us, to outwardly sing to a supreme being that theologically already knows the depths of the heart. There is the still body of certainty, sitting smugly in its chair, naysaying the special effects. And there is an aesthetic engagement with film and with ritual, the body that believes, that jumps in its seat when the killer emerges from the shadows, when the upbeat music erupts and the congregation rises to its feet.

II. The face, ethics and cinematics

The experience of cinema, like any ritual, is never simply a solitary experi-ence. It is, if anything, a kind of 'public intimacy' as Rachel Moore suggests (1999: 5). As the viewer becomes conscious of her or his aesthesiological body perceiving words and images, she or he also becomes conscious of the self's relation to, and dependence upon, others. A ritual, for all its aesthetic components, is never merely art for art's sake, but entails connections between one's self and one's body, and ultimately with other bodies in the world and includes a transformative aspect that is both interior and exterior to one's self. It is possible to see this movement in light of the ethical work of Emmanuel Levinas, particularly as he brings the ethical interaction with the other into a religious environment:

> Even when I shall have linked the Other to myself with the conjunction 'and' the Other continues to face me, to reveal himself in his face. *Religion* subtends this formal totality … Reflection can, to be sure, become aware of this face to face, but the 'unnatural' position of reflection is not an accident in the life of consciousness. It involves a calling into question of oneself, a critical attitude which is itself produced in face of the Other and under his authority. (1969: 80–1; emphasis in original)

What I am here suggesting is that experiences in film allow for a kind of 'face-to-face' encounter as described by Levinas, though in a more heightened way than Levinas ever seems to have thought. While Levinas's thought has been taken into the extremes of abstract, rational thinking, even to the point in which his central image of the 'face of the other' is only seen metaphorically, it is important to come back to the aesthetic face-to-face encounter itself. If Levinas claims ethics precedes ontology (the other precedes my-self), then we might rethink the manner in which the visual, material encounter with the face is actually an aesthetic encounter. Prior to the rational activity of visual categorisation (especially with regard to the race, ethnicity and gender of the other's face) is an aesthetic experience. Aesthetics precedes ethics.

Let us return to the visceral images of film. The face, particularly seen through the close-up, has been a continual focus, even obsession for filmmakers.[5] Entire film productions have been hung on individual actors' faces. As David MacDougall considers in ways that resonate with Levinas's ethics: 'In films the close-up creates a proximity to the faces and bodies of others that we experience much less commonly in daily life. The conventions of social distance normally restrict proximity except in moments of intimacy … The face is for most of us the locus of another person's being' (2006: 21). Continuing on and noting the presence of facial close-ups in films such as Carl Theodor Dreyer's *La Passion de Jeanne d'Arc* (*The Passion of Joan of Arc*, 1928) and Ingmar Bergman's *Persona* (1966) (to which I would add Lars von Trier's *Breaking the Waves*, 1996), MacDougall considers, 'The revelatory power of human faces resembles the revelatory power of film itself, which successively reveals new surfaces. Like the uncovering of the body and the release from social constraints that often accompanies it, film provides a sense of liberation that is fundamental to the magic, photogénie and underlying eroticism of the cinema' (2006: 22). By crossing the typical boundaries set in place by social custom (in Western societies we do not stand too close to other people and stare at their faces), films allow an experience with the face of an other that is not possible outside the theatre.

(This is also why I believe it is important for religious and ethical persons to seek out and view films that fall outside the Hollywood industrial system, as I have argued in more detail in other places.[6] For in the cinematic experience of commercial films the viewer is overwhelmingly subjected to the same kind of faces: white and male. Which is of course who the films are targeted towards.)

Because avant-garde film in particular does not rely on conventional cultural representations of the world, but engenders 'creative use of reality', in Maya Deren's phrase (1987: 60), the viewer sees something 'other', something potentially even non-recognisable. Usually what is non-recognisable has been right under our noses for a long time, only we have learned how not to see. The other-orientation of the avant-garde film can then lead to a new way of seeing and being in the world. No longer is the viewer reaffirmed in an objective, stable position, gazing at the other; rather, the subjectivity of the viewer is called into question. Deren suggests of the ritual process that there is a 'minimisation of personal identity' and through this minimisation comes a passage (a rite of passage) into a larger world outside of the self.[7]

One of the further consequences of this cinematic discipline of seeing is that it opens the way for a critical-ethical approach to cinema as a whole. I agree with Scott MacDonald who, in his book *Avant-Garde Film*, suggests that avant-garde films

> confront us with the necessity of redefining an experience we were
> sure we understood ... The experience provides us with the oppor-
> tunity (an opportunity much of our training has taught us to resist)
> to come to a clearer, more complete understanding of what the cin-

ematic experience actually can be, and what – for all the pleasure
and inspiration it may give us – the conventional movie experience
is *not*. (1993: 2; emphasis in original)

Religious cinematics is thus not merely a methodology, but contributes to
a larger ethical dimension. This ethical dimension is relevant for critical
approaches to film which attempt to bring forth issues of gender, sexuality,
race, ethnicity and class. Ideologies are always at play in viewing structures.

In the end, I do not wish to sound so naïvely optimistic (though maybe
a little so) as to imagine the world would be a better place if we all watched
avant-garde films more often, but there are strong ethical and transfor-
mational components involved, particularly as religious cinematics has
to do with our relations between others. Avant-garde film stands as a
strong alternative to the hegemony of the Hollywood film industry. Like
minimalism perhaps, and a few other artistic movements, but also like the
Buddhist orientation towards 'mindfulness', the religious cinematics of
viewing avant-garde films develops as a spiritual discipline (understanding 'spiritual' as indissociable from 'material'). By returning viewers to the
everyday through defamiliarisation and refamiliarisation, the cinematic
ritual of avant-garde film offers the possibility for aesthetic, ethical and
religious renewal.

III. Religious cinematics: seeing the dead body

By 'religious cinematics', I ultimately intend to indicate the activity of the
body, and the forces acting upon it, in a way related to religious ritual.
There are any number of theoretical definitions of ritual that could be
quoted here – from Victor Turner (1991) to Richard Schechner (1993), Mary
Douglas (1992) to Ronald Grimes (2000; 2006) – each with slight vari-
ants in their accents, but what is common across them is a stress on the
physicality of performance, of bodies engaging in symbolic actions, using
formalised speech, music and movement. Rituals act upon bodies, and
are likewise acted out *by* bodies. Transposing the physical into the human
sciences, we might say that ritual theory is a type of kinetics for the ways
in which it investigates performing bodies in accordance with the forces
of religious practice, tradition and belief. Specifically, I am thinking here

about the way the aesthesio-body moves in response to film. So on one level the cinematic experience has several parallels with religious ritual.

In a postindustrial, postmodern, information society, the cinematic experience supplements traditional ritual.[8] At the turn of the twentieth century, film became a magic medium, offering the possibility to re-enchant a Western world that increasingly explains itself away with scientific rigour. Soon after the invention of cinema Albert Einstein would elucidate how things in the physical world are not all they appear to be, as would Pablo Picasso and Georges Braque through artistic means, and Ferdinand de Saussure through linguistic means. Things do not appear as they are, nor say what they seem. In the wake of the development of cinema, filmmakers and film theorists responded to this situation, as Rachel Moore argues: 'The most striking and consistent concern of early film theory was the way modern language was seen as an impoverished expressive form whose arbitrariness and imprecision could be overcome by the moving picture' (1999: 7). If verbal language could be dissected and shown to have an inconsistent relation between signifier and signified, and if the physical world could be proved to actually operate in distinction to its appearance, moving images could step in and fill the representational gap, to demonstrate what is meant in relation to how it is represented. A train arriving at a station is exactly that, and so much so that viewers' bodies twitched and jumped in response. The cinematic experience promised a substitute for the traditional enchanting forces of ritual, offering ways – even if magical and ultimately unfulfilled – to get back to the underlying workings of the world itself. The gap in representation between event and the mediation of the event could be collapsed with film. (If this sounds strange, recall more contemporary promises of cable television and the Internet, where CNN's Headline News promises 'The world every half hour' and the World Wide Web promises just that, as if the whole world were enfolded in its grasp.)

At the turn of the twenty-first century, when the fully 'magic' possibilities of cinema have somewhat subsided, film nonetheless offers a reconnection to the workings of the world via ritual means. This is especially true in relation to that most critical of religious and ritual categories, the confrontation with death. In relation to rituals of death, contemporary societies are sorely *out of touch* with the body of death. As Philippe Ariès concludes in his study *Western Attitudes Toward Death*, 'In the modern period, death, despite the apparent continuity of themes and ritual, became challenged and was fur-

tively pushed out of the world of familiar things. In the realm of the imagination it became allied with eroticism in order to express the break with
the established order. In religion it signified … a scorn for the world and
an image of the void' (1974: 105–6). And the contemporary ritual theorist
Ronald Grimes states, 'Not only are we spiritually unprepared for whatever
hereafter there may be, most of us know little about what happens at death
in what our forbears used to call 'this' world. Even the mundane actions surrounding death – embalming a body, building a casket, cremating a corpse,
adapting a funeral rite – are foreign to us. Even though media and movies
traffic in death, only a few of us preplan funerals' (2000: 221). Death marks
a division between this world and the next, and in this way it can be pushed
aside, made as arbitrary as the verbal signifier, and even made 'invisible' as
Ariès suggests in his later study *The Hour of Our Death* (1987).

The following will focus on the ways in which the visible confrontation
with the dead body strikes the aesthetically perceiving body, and thereby
reawakens the senses (and ultimately perhaps the entire conscious
system). We will point towards a cinematic confrontation with the dead
body, and through the mediations of film and vision, the divisory dimensions of representation are broken down. I take the importance of the two
mediators of film and sense receptors discussed above, and look towards
their dissolution in the ultimate religio-technological quest: the desire for
an unmediated experience with the world, a quest that is finally the quest
for transcendence of the world. The paradox is well noted: the quest to get
beyond media is achieved in and through media.

Stan Brakhage, like many in the avant-garde, continued to work
towards a 'magical' mode of filmmaking in the twentieth century, not by
going back before the Enlightenment to some pure, innocent and/or pre-
scientific place, but through a retrained perception, enabling a transcendent experience in and through media. Brakhage makes the link between
the religious and the filmic clear: 'Suppose the Vision of the saint and the
artist to be an increased ability to see – vision' (1978: 120). When a ritual
is edited and turned into a film, watchable in one sitting, time and space
are compressed and reconfigured, and the viewer experiences a relation
between, for example, death and life in a new form. Not only is the oscil-
lation between death and life at the centre of many traditional rituals, but
the reconfiguration of space and time into a singular aesthetic experience
is also a key trait of ritual. As avant-garde filmmaker Maya Deren states: 'A

ritual is an action distinguished from all others in that it seeks the realisation of its purpose through the exercise of form. In this sense ritual is art; and even historically, all art derives from ritual. Being a film ritual, it is achieved not in spatial terms alone, but in terms of Time created by the camera' (1965: 6). Film production records and reinvents time and space themselves, offering new perspectives on the sacred and profane, the fabulous and mundane, life and death.

Brakhage was obsessed with 'birth, sex, death and the search for God', and in his filmic approaches to death, he also turned to the search for God and the dead body, wanting to see all of it as if for the first time. The dead, unmoving body is transposed through his camera which is then perceived by the cinematic body of the film viewer. One of the best examples here may be his *Sirius Remembered* (1959) where, in the search to create a meaningful new symbol of death because the old inherited symbols had lost their value, Brakhage placed the body of his deceased dog, Sirius, in the woods near his house and filmed the corpse at various stages of decomposition over several seasons. Rather than being the gruesome spectacle that many in modern, sanitised society might expect after such a description, the film creates a beautiful and loving rite of mourning and meaning-making out of death, and the relation to the mutable, fallible body. 'This is an age which has no symbol for death', Brakhage claimed in the early 1960s, 'other than the skull and bones of one stage of decomposition ... and it is an age which lives in fear of total annihilation' (1978: 121). Seeking a new image of death, a way to experience it before the abstractions of the 'logical' body, Brakhage's camera intrudes into and crosses the line between death and life. 'Suddenly', he recalls on the death of his dog, 'I was faced in the centre of my life with the death of a loved being which tended to undermine all my abstract thoughts of death' (in Sitney 2002: 172).

Nowhere is the confrontation with death more immediate than in his film, *The Act of Seeing With One's Own Eyes*. The title refers to the literal signification of 'autopsy', and the film consists of 31 minutes of silent footage of autopsies shot in a Pittsburgh morgue. Bodies are cut into, cut apart, opened up, skin peeled back, organs removed and measured, until there is almost nothing left that resembles a human body. Many of Brakhage's films, as is true of other avant-garde filmmakers, tend to work on an abstract, even mythical level, rarely engaging with the historical world. This film, to the contrary, 'anchors itself to the historical world relentlessly' (Nichols

1991: 79). *The Act of Seeing* confronts the cinematic body with a 'real' body. This is strikingly distinct from the thousands of fictional dead bodies we see in films all the time. In fiction films, the death (fictive death) is portrayed with conventional symbolic actions: usually something like a close-up of the dying victim taking his last gasp of breath while lying in the lover's arms, revealing the deep secret of his life, as the heavily-stringed musical score crescendos. Such a representation of death, Vivian Sobchack suggests, 'does not move us to inspect it' (2004: 235). We remain sated in our seats, understanding the necessity of death within the film's narrative; sad perhaps, but there is little offering to actually think or feel our way through death itself. However, 'while death is generally experienced in fiction films as representable and often excessively visible, in documentary films it is experienced as confounding representation, as exceeding visibility' (ibid.). Because a majority of us 'moderns' have seen hundreds more fictional, represented deaths than actual deaths, our eyes have been trained to see death in particular ways. A display of real death then breaks into our aesthetically constructed world and our bodies do not know what to do with it. We writhe, turn away, feel our stomach churn, walk away. Brakhage's film is excessive and resists symbolising and narrativising. We have the rational capacity to deal with represented death (often becoming cathartic), but we are rarely given the structures to face real death. 'As excess, the by-products of mechanical vision defy the containment of the work and are more capable of touching the exposed sensibilities of the viewer' (MacDougall 2005: 18). What we are left with is the cinematic body reacting to the dead and dissected body. The moving body of observation reacts and responds to the still body that is being acted upon by coroners.

The clinical approach of the coroners in the film may be somewhat disturbing (they move on the bodies like a car mechanic on a transmission), but Brakhage's camera remains strikingly non-judgmental, indeed, clinical. He is careful not to reveal the faces, and therefore the identities, of the dead bodies. Interestingly, the faces of the coroners performing the autopsies are shown only twice: a custodian's face is seen as he cleans up after, and at the very end a coroner is shown in a pure-white, cadaver-free room speaking his report into a recorder. We understand the necessity of performing autopsies, so the activity itself cannot be thought of as unethical. Here is Enlightenment science, with its removal of magic, its pure dissection, objectifying what is most feared.

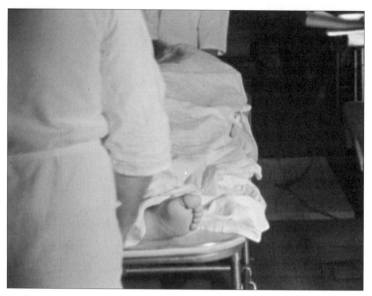

Faceless coroners, working on bodies like car mechanics on transmissions in *The Act of Seeing with One's Own Eyes*

Anthropologist Michael Taussig has recently considered the power of 'defacement' as a mode of understanding how the despoiling of something beautiful and/or sacred can in itself become mysterious and thus reaffirm the sacred. Related to certain societies' ritual acts of 'unmasking', Taussig also links defacement to the activities of contemporary art, including film. He quotes from Thomas Elsaesser on editing: 'It is the cut as the montage principle that makes the energy in the system visible and active' (Taussig 1999: 4). There is a hidden magic that is brought into the open, but its liberation often requires the violence of defacing, cutting, desecrating or splicing in the editing room. The act of defacement, 'brings insides outside, unearthing knowledge and revealing mystery. As it does this, however, as it spoliates and tears at tegument, it may also animate the thing defaced and the mystery revealed may become more mysterious, indicating the curious magic upon which Enlightenment, in its elimination of magic, depends' (ibid.). Film, on such an account, in its carving up of space and time, of taking apart the seemingly seamless beauty of the 'world as it is', transgresses a natural order and is therefore de-creative. But in this activity it unearths other mysteries. The Enlightenment's visual technologies brought the cosmos closer. Attempting to chart the workings of the universe, new tools were created to see better and clearer, to demonstrate that it was not magic at the heart of the workings of the world but rather natural causes and effects. And yet, in these discoveries, before the rational body describes its new chartings and categories for the ways things work, there is the aesthetic body that has simply seen and moved in response.

Film technology has acquired the tools of Enlightenment science and turned the findings into a spectacle to be sure, but film has also shown this re-found world to a mass audience, eager to see new things in new ways. Film allows a fresh perspective on the world, a different way of viewing material structures and events. Conceptions of the way the world works are dramatically different at the beginning of the twenty-first century than they were at the beginning of the twentieth, due in part to the influence of film. From Eadweard Muybridge's photographic experiments with bodies in motion to Dziga Vertov's reconstruction of the city in *Man with a Movie Camera* to Stanley Kubrick's reconsideration of space and technology in *2001: A Space Odyssey* (1968), filmmakers have recreated the 'reality' of the world, allowing viewers a new way of looking and ultimately conceptualising the world around them. By offering a vision of everyday life in an innovative, challenging way, film changes the perceptions of the familiar. As Walter Benjamin suggested, what were once overlooked structures – 'our bars and city streets, our offices and furnished rooms, our railroad stations and our factories' – are brought into a new focus, from a new angle. Benjamin continues: 'With the close-up, space expands; with slow motion, movement is extended. And ... enlargement not merely clarifies what we see indistinctly "in any case", but brings to light entirely new structures of matter' (2002: 117). The world is perceived anew, leading to a reconstructed 'worldview'. Here the metaphorical language of world*view* must be broken down in order to see the ways vision is a constructor of worlds, that it plays a prominent role in worldmaking enterprises, and that film has become a key broker in the activity of worldmaking in the contemporary age.

This, I suggest, gets at what Brakhage's film revives. And nowhere is this truer than during the few occasions where the camera gazes for lengthy periods of time on a human face that is slowly being peeled back from the top of the head to the nose, allowing the coroners access to the skull and ultimately the brain. The body is literally defaced, and through such activity the mysteries of the human brain – this soft spongy stuff responsible for tremendous acts of creation, invention and destruction – is revealed. Even with all the advances of science we really know little about how this bodily substance can produce activity in the world. This gap in knowledge, then, between inhabited body and knowledge about that body, is the curious magic. It is one thing to write this, but another to see it.

The film may be the most literal rendition of Benjamin's analogy of the medium of filmmaking as compared to the older visualising practice of painting: 'Magician is to surgeon as painter is to cinematographer. The painter maintains in his work a natural distance from reality, whereas the cinematographer penetrates deeply into its tissue' (2002: 116). What is revealed is 'another nature', one not accessible to the social life of the status quo. The camera offers glimpses into another world – outer space, outer Mongolia, or the inner cavity of the body. 'With all its resources for swooping and rising, disrupting and isolating, stretching and compressing a sequence, enlarging or reducing an object', the camera brings us to 'discover the optical unconscious, just as we discover the instinctual unconscious through psychoanalysis' (2002: 117). Brakhage's camera collapses Benjamin's analogy, penetrating into the body.

The Act of Seeing strikes at primal fears: the fear of invasion of one's own body, the fear of contact with the dead body, the fear of death itself. In bringing insides outside, in crossing the boundaries between death and life, the viewer transgresses socially imposed divisions. Social divisions keep the pure and impure separate, and little fits these categories better than the difference between life and death. All that is associated with death is to be kept, literally, 'out of sight' in the modern, civilised society. Thomas Laquer explains this well:

> Corporal politics – making manifest the body in all its vulnerable, disarticulated, morbid aspects, in its apertures, curves, protuberances where the boundaries between self and the world are porous – is somehow indecent. 'It is in keeping as far as possible out of sight, not only actual pain, but all that can be offensive or disagreeable to the most sensitive person, that refinement exists', writes the great liberal philosopher John Stuart Mill. In fact, it is a sign

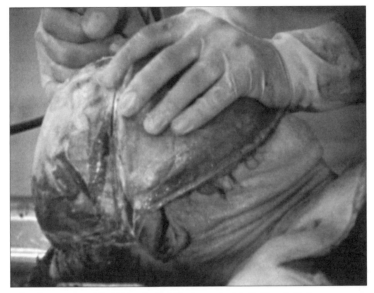

Defaced corpses reveal the hidden depths of the human body in Brakhage's filming

of the 'high state of civilisation', of the 'perfection of mechanical arrangements', that so much can be kept hidden ... The infliction of pain, as Mill points out, is delegated 'to the judge, the soldier, the surgeon, the butcher, the executioner'. (1992: 14)[9]

Brakhage's film offers the opportunity to be uncivilised, to reclaim a magic relation to one's own body, to see with one's own eyes. To be moved, not to rational knowledge, but to a corporeal response that may be no response at all, is the effect of the immediate experience to the religious cinematic experience.

4   THE FOOTPRINTS OF FILM: AFTER-IMAGES OF RELIGION IN SPACE AND TIME

In front of Philadelphia's stately Museum of Art – with its extensive, well-respected collections of Asian and American works – one can find the footprints of Rocky Balboa at the top of the great steps. Tourists from all over the world have made mini-pilgrimages here as they climb the enormous stairway leading to the museum and the footprints, a little hunk of cement with its indents of Rocky's Converse high tops. Jumping up and down with arms raised, these tourist-pilgrims have their photograph taken, then they will go home and put that image in their scrapbooks and on web pages to say, 'Look, I stood where Rocky stood!' 'Rocky', as many will remember, refers here to 'Rocky Balboa', the character played by Sylvester Stallone in the *Rocky* films (1976–2006). While Grauman's Chinese Theatre in Hollywood is well known for its footprints and handprints of famous movie stars in the walkway outside, the impressions there are accompanied by the actors' real names, people who have actual hands that can make an imprint in setting cement. But in the case of Rocky's footprints, we realise there is no 'Rocky', he was only a fictional character in a movie.[1]

The religious landscape of the US is littered with just such footprints of film. Far from being immaterial – nothing but light projected on a two-dimensional surface – filmic images have leapt off the screen and entered physical, three-dimensional spaces, leaving their marks in American cement, religious consciousness and ritual practices. Like the character Tom Baxter in Woody Allen's *The Purple Rose of Cairo*, film has stepped

The contemporary pilgrimage: footprints of the fictional character 'Rocky' at the top of the
Philadelphia Museum of Art await real people to stand in them

down from the screen to infiltrate political, social and religious lives. The
argument here is that religion and film leave the temples and theatres,
synagogues and living rooms, and meet in the streets, stairways, parking
lots, weddings, funerals, cities and deserts of the US.

The aim of this chapter is to triangulate the religion-film relation
to make a larger argument for the ways in which filmed characters and
scenarios have come down off the screen and entered the religious landscapes of present-day society and contemporary ritualising practices. This
triangulation works to delineate a space, literally and metaphorically, in
which religion and film meet in the US religious geography. We shall see
how films have influenced contemporary rituals such as weddings and
funerals, bar mitzvahs and baptisms, and the ways they have constructed
brand new rituals as is the case with cult movies such as *The Rocky Horror
Picture Show* (1975). At times rituals must be reinvented, at other times
they are built from the ground up, and media such as film are integral to
the ever-evolving cultural systems of religious traditions.

I. Ritualising films

Recently, as part of a weekly response to class readings, one of my students discussed how her brother had chosen *Matrix*-style clothing – leather trench-coats, sunglasses and so forth – for his wedding. I have seen the *Matrix* trilogy on many occasions, have shown *The Matrix* to my classes every year for the past five years and read a lot about the films.[2] I know there are a lot of aficionados (or cult followers, depending on how you phrase it) of these films, but until I read my student's paper I had not thought about the ways it leaves its own formal confines and infiltrates the lives and ritual structures of average US citizens. This provoked me to think further about how films have impacted on rituals and I did some research on film and ritual in the US.[3]

According to an article in *Bride's* magazine from September 2001, 'theme weddings', including those based on films, are a hot trend in the wedding industry. Many wedding planning guides offer a variety of focal themes, from Renaissance to underwater weddings, from Hawaiian to Scottish to fairy tale lands, and the ever-popular Elvis impersonator pre-siding. Online sites offer a plethora of theme wedding packages includ-ing Roaring '20s, Disney, *Star Trek* and the 'Hollywood theme' which one online wedding planner describes this way:

> As your white limo whispers to a halt before the expectant crowd, the handsome man at your side smiles lovingly into your eyes. You step gracefully from the car, your diamonds sparkling with every movement. ('Diamonds' are a state of mind!) You pause as a mass of avid fans and photographers surround you, begging a moment of your precious time. Magnanimously, you scrawl your autograph and casually tilt your head for the snapshot of the century. (First making sure your good side is towards the camera, of course!) Finally, clinging possessively to your leading man, you reluctantly tear yourself away from your adoring fans and head for the elabo-rate reception that is being held in your honour.
> Is this all just a dream? No, this could be your wedding![4]

The site 'Wedding Shops Online' offers suggestions of wedding themes like 'country/western', 'ethnic', 'nautical' and 'Movie or Television'.

For the latter they give the idea: 'Have all in attendance dress up as characters from your favourite movie or television programme (i.e. *Star Trek*). Carry the theme throughout the reception – serve food that was served during the movie, play theme music, etc. Send invitation and programme designed as a "Play Bill".'[5] Other Internet searches reveal couples having theme weddings based on films such as *Gone with the Wind*, *Casablanca* and *Braveheart*. And lovetripper.com, a resource for honeymoon planning, offers a list of 'romantic movie quotes' to 'spice up your love letters', including one-liners from *The Bridges of Madison County* ('This kind of certainty comes but once in a lifetime'), *West Side Story* ('Goodnight, goodnight, sleep well and when you dream, dream of me...') and *Crouching Tiger, Hidden Dragon* ('A faithful heart makes wishes come true').[6]

Similar movie themes can be created for b'nai mitzvahs (mitzvoth). Indeed, Woody Allen's film *Deconstructing Harry* (1997) depicts a *Star Wars*-themed bar mitzvah, complete with a child cutting the cake with a light sabre. Yet, the scene did not stem wholly from the imaginative mind of Allen, but can be seen in life itself. The online partypop.com offers suggestions and planning for bar mitzvahs with themes from films such as *Back to the Future*, *The Terminator* and *Lost in Space*. The online sales pitch tells us the story of 'Marcus' who recently had a *Terminator*-theme for his coming of age party/ritual:

> Everything in the hall looked like metal ... There were even jungle gyms and slides painted in camouflage colours for them to play on. Once everyone had arrived, the Aliea La Tora [sic] was performed on the hall stage. Then, since everyone was already in the hall, Marcus's grand entrance was a ride around the hall in an electric scooter decorated to look like the Terminator's motorcycle in T2. It was his bar mitzvah gift from his parents. Marcus got on and made a victory lap while the DJ played the *Terminator* theme music.[7]

Or note Lisa Niren's *Titanic*-themed bat mitzvah, reported by the Associated Press:

> Thirteen-year-old Lisa Niren, described by her sister as obsessed with *Titanic*, got the bat mitzvah of her dreams over the weekend.

A hotel ballroom was transformed into the luxury liner, with 12-foot steaming smokestacks at the buffet table, phosphorescent artificial icebergs and a 'steerage' section for the children ...

The *pièce de résistance* was a gigantic photo, 10 feet above the floor, featuring Lisa's face superimposed over actress Kate Winslet's body in a famous *Titanic* scene on the prow of the ocean liner. Lisa appeared to have teen heartthrob Leonardo DiCaprio smiling over her shoulder ...

Reflective aqua-tinted lighting along the walls and the phosphorescent blue and green icebergs made it appear as if the ballroom was under water.

Tables featured roses, crystal candelabras and replicas of the heart-shaped blue diamond necklace from the movie.

'This is incredible', said Heather Levy, a friend of Lisa's mother. 'A lot of people do things for their children because they love them, but this goes beyond all that. I'm just standing here smiling.' (Anon. 1998)

Granted, such b'nai mitzvahs and weddings make up a small but growing percentage of all ceremonies conducted in the US, yet their existence indicates some of the ways young people and couples are searching for ways to 'personalise' their rituals.

And plenty of other religious services realise this need for the updating of media and are happily incorporating film into their liturgies. This seems to be particularly true among evangelical Christian churches. In fact, it seems that the more conservative a church is theologically the less problem it has pulling down a screen in the middle of a Sunday morning sermon and playing a clip from a film. Meanwhile the mainline Protestant and Roman Catholic churches tend to relegate film to the Adult Education courses on Sunday mornings or Wednesday nights.[8]

Moving in the opposite direction, the influence of the audio-visual, technological *recordability* of rituals has undoubtedly been observed by anyone who has attended a wedding, b'nai mitzvah, baptism, ordination or funeral in the past ten years. These rituals are often overwhelmed by the presence of uncles, fathers, friends or even professionals hired for the event who 'memorialise' the ritual through their latest techno-gizmos (there is an interesting element of masculinity to much of this visual techno-gazing/recording).[9] Memory, perhaps the central facet of ritual, is produced in and through media, and the so-called reality of the memory is deeply dependent on the medium through which it exists, whether that is a verbal medium (such as spoken or printed word), visual medium (such as a photograph) or is multimedia (film, performance and so forth).

This is not the place for a thorough ethnographic study of film-themed rituals here, but I note their existence and again mark the ways film has left an imprint on contemporary ritualising processes. There will be plenty of critics here who see these rites of passage as succumbing to entertainment and consumerism, one more step in the commodification and secularisation of religious traditions. And there may be a lot to the charge. But there is more to it than that.

My student whose *Matrix*-inspired brother re-outfitted his matrimonial wardrobe had been reading Ronald Grimes' thoughtful work, *Deeply into the Bone: Re-Inventing Rites of Passage* (2000). Grimes plays with the possibilities of having renewed rituals to keep us contemporary humans inspired, to give us meaning in the patterns of our lives and to connect within a society that too often produces alienation. Throughout his book, Grimes is concerned with what seems to be a growing absence of rites of passage in the modern age, and offers an interesting, if not extreme, quote from the *Encyclopedia of World Problems and Human Potential*: 'The absence of rites of passage leads to a serious breakdown in the process of maturing as a person. Young people are unable to participate in society in a creative manner because societal structures no longer consider it their responsibility to intentionally establish the necessary marks of passing from one age-related social role to another' (in Grimes 2000: 91). Humans have an ongoing need for ritual, as many have suggested, but Grimes also raises the concern that 'traditional rites themselves can become so ethereal that they fail to connect with the bodily realities and spiritual needs of those who undergo them' (2000: 100). And this is where the need for re-invented rites becomes so important. The *Matrix* marriage had an air of novelty to it, but perhaps was a way to lighten what some felt was an overly solemn occasion (after all, marriage should be fun so why not relax a little). Perhaps it is the assumed solemnity of the occasions that produce alienation and disconnection and new media create a sense of lightness and approachability.

Since a Jewish boy is automatically a bar mitzvah at age 13 and a girl at age 12 is automatically a bat mitzvah, with or without the ritual, perhaps the theme of the festivities is not important. But others *do* see it all as intertwined. Concerned with the stodgy old ways of creating bar/bat mitzvah rituals and parties, Gail Greenberg recently wrote a popular book and created a company called 'MitzvahChic'. She says: 'Since the 1950s b'nai mitzvah have followed the same formula and *nothing* has changed except which trendy themes are in vogue. But now, we recognise that there's *got* to be more, that we've exhausted the thrills and satisfaction we can get through decorating and the old routines alone.' Greenberg, and it seems many others who have heeded her advice, realises there is still power in ritual, and without much scholarly knowledge of ritual studies, she seems to implicitly know that a re-invention of rituals is vital to religious tradition. Not wholly advocating the throwing out of tradition, nor simply suggesting anything goes, the 'MitzvahChic' approach attempts to bring the deep significance of the older traditions together with personal meaning in a contemporary age: 'Today's bar mitzvah/bat mitzvah has a new level of spirituality; new ways of adding tzedakah, having fun and making it beautiful.'[10] The *Terminator* theme noted earlier may have questionable meaning-making abilities (a victory lap in an electric scooter!) but the need for personal connection in ritual is very real.

As quantified evidence for the role of popular media in the shaping of contemporary religiosity, Lynn Schofield Clark has offered a number of intriguing studies on media and adolescent religious identity in the US. Her book *From Angels to Aliens: Teenagers, the Media and the Supernatural* (2003), based on hundreds of interviews with teenagers and their families, demonstrates how many youth today express their own understanding of 'religion', 'spirituality' and the 'supernatural' through media symbols. Television shows such as *The X Files* (1993–2002) and *Buffy the Vampire Slayer* (1997–2003), along with films such as *The Sixth Sense* (1999) and the *Harry Potter* franchise (2001–2007), provide articulations for the ways US teens understand themselves to be 'religious'. Clark suggests:

> A great deal of evidence suggests that the media play an important role in how young people form and articulate their identities. Young people learn from and identify with characters they watch and with celebrities they admire. Their choices for media consumption have a lot to do with the identifications they hold according to their participation in different racial, class, gender and friend-

ship groups ... Given the significance of the entertainment media
in the lives of teens, it's worth exploring what teens mean when
they identify themselves as religious, and what such identifica-
tions might have to do with what they see, hear and consume in
the media. (2003: 17)

Among other interesting findings, Clark's work demonstrates how the
secularisation thesis has not taken account of the role of media in actively
shaping what can only be called religious views of US culture. While non-
traditional religious movements are replacing 'traditional' religious institutions, media such as film, television, comic books and video games are
replacing traditional institutional worldviews with new articulations, new
descriptions and depictions of very old religious categories like good and
evil, sin, angels, demons and God.

Ritualising and world-building are necessary to religion, but the same
old ritual in the same old way, the same old message in the same old
medium, leaves people feeling disconnected. Central to re-ritualising processes is the necessity of attention to the media of transmission. From oral-
ity to literacy, printing presses to the Internet, 'tradition' becomes abstract
and stale if everyone repeats the same things in rote manner through the
same medium. To invent new and meaningful rites many people now turn
to film (and other forms of media such as television, comic books and
games) to help them through stages of life. These media have become
familiar, comfortable. In many instances it may be just good clean fun,
but in other very real ways films offer linguistic and symbolic registers and
ways of understanding the world from vital, new perspectives, touching
on sensual aspects that words alone are too limited to deal with.

II. Creating new rituals: from rocky to rocky horror

New media alter old rituals, but they also produce brand new rituals, in
places and times the traditionally-minded religious person would not
think to look. At the time of writing this, thousands of people were camping on the streets – a notable few had been camping for months – waiting
for the tickets to go on sale for the final instalment of the *Star Wars* series.
These fans were dressed in *Star Wars*-specific costumes, spending time
with friends along the way, just to be able to participate in that special,

set-apart time and place where they could watch *Star Wars: Episode III – Revenge of the Sith* (2005). The 'religion' of *Star Wars* has often been noted in popular and scholarly literature alike, and a Romanian-based fan club has just opened the first known 'Jedi Academy'.[11] Indeed, in the 2001 Australian national census, over 70,000 people marked 'Jedi' as their religion, hoping to get it listed as an official religion recognised by the nation. Responding to this religious/political movement, Chris Brennan, director of the *Star Wars* Appreciation Society of Australia, stated, 'This was a way for people to say, "I want to be part of a movie universe I love so much"' (see Taggart 2001). Brennan's words are telling, especially when compared to Jonathan Z. Smith's definition of ritual: 'Ritual is a means of performing the way things *ought to be* in conscious tension to the way things are in such a way that this ritualised perfection is recollected in the ordinary, uncontrolled, course of things' (1982: 63; emphasis added). *Star Wars* fans re-enact and recollect an alternate reality – standing in line for days and weeks, dressing the part, being with like-costumed and like-minded people, *participating* in a world (both on the streets outside the theatre and as part of the filmed world onscreen) that expresses 'the way things ought to be' – a reality in contradistinction to the humdrum existence of office spaces, mortgage instalments and traffic jams.

Perhaps no other film, blockbuster or otherwise, has created a greater ritualised following than *The Rocky Horror Picture Show*. While many religious studies scholars might write off this film as a campy production with little ethical or religious value, it has nonetheless elicited a mass, cult following since its debut. The plot line is a retelling of an old story, with the bourgeoisie (represented by Brad and Janet – played by Barry Bostwick and Susan Sarandon) encountering another, alternate social reality (here at the underworldly castle-home of Dr Frank N. Furter – Tim Curry) and being transformed by the experience. 'Normal' social behaviour is mocked throughout the film; polymorphous perversions and various acts of violence (the reason it is a 'horror show'), including cannibalism, are demonstrated onscreen, turning Brad and Janet's 'traditional' values upside down. They are transformed through their experiences. The plot itself relates to Victor Turner's (following Van Gennep's) tri-partite schema of religious ritual entailing: separation, liminality, reincorporation. But it is in the watching of the film where the true religious dimensions surface, as it *functions* religiously by way of audience interaction, as they also go through the three-part ritual process.[12] Now, thirty years after its creation, in almost any major city across the United States and elsewhere, at the liminal hour of Saturday midnight, one can find a screening and a devoted crowd of people still gathering, donning costumes related to the film, along with their special 'props'. A fair number of people have now seen the film over 1,000 times. Those who have previously never attended a screening are termed 'virgins' (and often are made to wear a lipsticked 'V' on their foreheads). Indeed, an entire vocabulary has been developed in relation to the screenplay.

In their article, 'Toward a Sociology of Cult Films: Reading *Rocky Horror*', Patrick Kinkade and Michael Katovich explore the phenomenon of secular filmic cult audiences. Drawing on previous work in the field, they define 'cult film audiences' as 'a type of secular cult organisation, and cultish attachments to these films replace a charismatic actor with a document granted charismatic appeal' (1992: 192). Such a definition is intriguing for the ways in which it redefines traditional central sacred texts and figures, implicitly noting the ways in which media affect what can only be called 'piety'. As Kinkade and Katovich continue, cult film audiences, 'construct ritual and belief systems through their viewing experience. Cult film attachments, therefore, become obsessions and enduring shared foci for habitues' (1992: 194).[13]

Such behavioural systems are readily apparent at screenings of *The Rocky Horror Picture Show*, as audience members enact ritual activities in tandem with other audience members and in conjunction with the film scenes. In the film theatre, audience members perform events that mimic the events onscreen: the audience throws rice at the point when Brad and Janet get married at the beginning of the film; and people bring actual toast with them so at the point when Frank N. Furter proposes a 'toast', the audience throws their toast at the screen. These responses have been repeated and codified over the years, so that now one can attend a screening across the world and encounter the same performative actions. Cult audiences, including those often seen at screenings of *The Rocky Horror Picture Show*, are often comprised of disenfranchised members of society who find connection, meaning and solace within such liminal activities as a form of 'spontaneous communitas' is formed.

One could easily and cynically ask here: how many seemingly grass-roots responses are in fact created as publicity stunts? Mel Gibson's *The Passion of the Christ* is a clear demonstration of how this can happen, and while it has become one of the top-grossing films of all time, it seems to have done so by mimicking the disenfranchised aspects of the cult film phenomenon: Gibson as outsider who must fund his film by himself (the fact that he *could* come up with the $30 million by himself should probably alert us to the fact that he was anything but an outsider), the Hollywood industry that shuns him, reviewers that pan the film, just as the film ostensibly tells the story of a social outsider pushed down by the socio-religious authorities. Just as Gibson and his marketing people clearly promoted the film as Hollywood insiders who know the code, in like manner, advertisers and theatre managers probably sparked the *Rocky Horror* cult.[14] Thus, at a certain point one might be tempted to suggest that there is some 'pure' grass-roots ritual process standing in contrast to these 'artificial' commercial constructions.

But rituals, like culture in general, are always a production (however ongoing and morphing) made up by the webs of significance of economics, social life, legal issues, cultural symbols, human bodies, religious institutions, communal interactions and personal beliefs. I am not suggesting that some films offer 'pure' rituals, stemming from the untainted underground life of the disenfranchised, while others are merely industry standards. Rather, I am suggesting again that religion and film meet in a much larger and more diverse US social and cultural milieu than has heretofore been suggested by scholars working in the field.

In Clifford Geertz's well-known definition, religion offers symbols, powerful and pervasive moods and motivations, as it formulates 'conceptions of a general order of existence', arranging all of this to seem 'uniquely realistic' (1973: 90). Through special effects, editing, cinematography and finely honed acting, films and their reception offer much of the same. The trailers at the cinema even tell us as much. As we sit down with our popcorn – perhaps dressed as a stormtrooper or a Wookie – waiting for the feature presentation, we hear the voiceover for the coming attractions: 'In a world where you have to fight to be free…'; 'In a world where love is within reach…'; 'In a world…'. We the viewers are invited into other worlds, alternate renditions of reality that through seamless editing, precise special effects, carefully placed cameras and elaborate props offer views of the world that seem 'uniquely realistic'. Film, like religion, tells of another reality, of a world that could be, of a world that viewers want to live in – or in the case of apocalyptic films a world viewers want to avoid. Regardless, films present other realities that stimulate moods and motivations.[15] One way or another, film viewers have their eyes and ears opened to differing ways of imagining the world outside the film theatre, but also outside our own social status in the world 'out there'. In the audio-visual experience of viewing film, human bodies and minds have an experience that becomes internalised, ultimately affecting behaviours, attitudes, practices and beliefs. And we often find the experience of film somehow transformed, translated and transposed into the granite structures, the cement surfaces and Saturday night haunts that constitute contemporary religious life.

Conclusion

To conclude, I leave one final footprint. In Austin, Texas, between the state's capitol and judicial buildings, there is a 6ft x 3ft granite sculpture of the Ten Commandments, chiselled in a quasi-Gothic script (in King James English of course), with decorative flourishes – the Christic Greek chi-ro characters, Stars of David and an American flag – surrounding the words. This 'monument' was erected in 1961 and my research reveals little interest in it since that time. But in the early twenty-first century, the Austin sculpture has become one of many contested sites in the US in which church-state relations have been put to the test. The case went all the way to the US Supreme Court on the grounds that such a presentation entails the government endorsing religion, while conservative lawmakers argue for the ways in which these commandments pay tribute to the religious and legal history of the US.[16]

What neither side rarely admits – or simply remains ignorant of the history of these sculptures – is that the plethora of Ten Commandments sculptures outside courthouses, capitols and urban squares in the US today actually came into being through the publicity stunts of the great filmmaker, Cecil B. DeMille. In the mid-1950s, DeMille was finishing his second version of *The Ten Commandments* (1956), famously starring Charlton Heston as Moses. As promotion for the film, DeMille got in touch with the Fraternal Order of Eagles (FOE), a nationwide association of civic-minded clubs (founded in 1898, interestingly enough, by a group of theatre owners), who had been distributing copies of the Ten Commandments to courtrooms across the country as 'guidance' for juvenile delinquents. DeMille and the FOE upped the symbolic stability of the Decalogue by com-

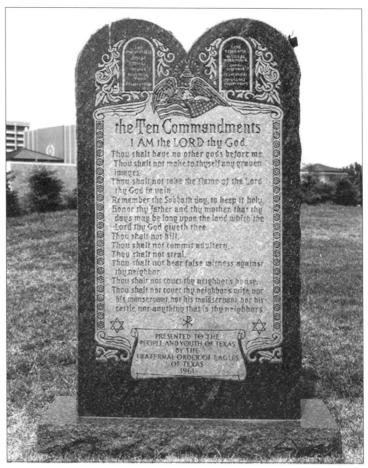

The vestiges of Cecile B. DeMille's publicity stunts for *The Ten Commandments:* across the US, sculptures remain near courthouses

missioning hundreds of granite sculptures of Moses' tablets to be placed outside courthouses across the US, including Austin, Texas. DeMille died in 1959, but the FOE continued the task of planting the sculptures through the 1960s, and they are now the focal point of Supreme Court decisions that impinge directly on church-state issues in the United States.[17]

Film has left its footprints in US culture, society, political discourse and religious consciousness. These footprints are not those of abstract thought, but of material structures in physical time and space. Film progresses from its two-dimensional, light-projected status, to incarnated, three-dimensional aspects. And the point at which it becomes so interesting is when it is realised that film has so permeated cultural consciousness that people forget how material 'reality' can have its origins in ethereal light projected onto a screen. There is no 'Rocky', and granite Ten Commandments are as much vestigial publicity stunts as they are making a statement about God-given law being the origin of the modern legal system. The image is confused for the real, and we realise therein that the real is always already imagined, and often primarily imaged.

In the contemporary United States, film is no longer existent only in celluloid, or even in digital code. Film has left the movie theatre, infiltrated old rituals and fashioned new ones. It has made its marks in cement, and these concrete places become, in turn, an alluring topography that attracts people to them. Film merges into the public spaces of civic life as it engenders court cases promoting deep political dialogue that harkens back to the founding of the nation, long before the moving, refracted-light image was a twinkle in the eyes of the Lumière brothers or Thomas Edison.

NOTES

preface

1   This paragraph is a highly condensed history of a richer conversation that
    has been taken up by several recent scholars; see the much fuller his-
    tories of the interdiscipline found in Lyden (2003: 11–35); Plate (2004a:
    3097–103); and Wright (2006: 11–32). Also, the most comprehensive
    bibliography of the field to date can be found in Mitchell & Plate (2007).
2   A short list of this third wave would also include Lyden 2003; Marsh
    2004; Wright 2006; and Johnston 2007.

introduction

1   Abraham Heschel is paraphrasing the Zohar here.
2   See also Walter Benjamin's suggestions (2002: 117) and my own com-
    ments on the subject (2005: 105–12).
3   The philosopher Stanley Cavell was way ahead of some of this argument as
    he turned to the projections of film as a way of understanding the world.
    His book *The World Viewed* (1979) argues that the world as it is holds a
    distinct relation to the 'world viewed' onscreen, and that the two are not
    entirely distinguishable, even if the screened world goes out of existence
    when the film is over. Yet, just below the surface of Cavell's writings is a
    suggestion that cinema is ultimately a private, anonymous experience.
4   These levels are quoted in Warren Buckland (2000: 47); see also
    Etienne Souriau (1953). Souriau's work has not been translated into
    English, but good overviews include chapter 3 of Edward Lowry's *The
    Filmology Movement and Film Study in France* (1985).

5   I am referring to books by Christopher Hitchens, Richard Dawkins, Sam Harris, Daniel Dennett and others. Overall, I am quite sympathetic with their complaints about religion (and one of the problems with teaching and writing about religion is that we have to continually face the paradoxical situation as to how religion both poisons *and* cures everything – to borrow from a subtitle by Hitchens), but for the most part these writers fail to understand what religion is all about. Their approach is intellectual, in the head, failing to grasp the bodily dimensions – indeed, bases – of religion.

chapter one

1   On the relation of films and myths, Tim Burton says 'I grew up loving movies. So I realise that I love the mythology, folk tale kind of thing … because that's basically what movies are as well … They were just variations on all the kind of classic imagery that way, and symbols' (in Schwartz 2005: 177). For more on the film and especially the book on which it was based in relation to myth, see William Doty's 'Myths and Tales in Big Fish', in *Mythic Passages*, December 2006. This is available at: http://www.mythicjourneys.org/newsletter_dec06_doty.html (accessed 15 March 2008).
2   While there is no space to elaborate on fuller definitions of myth, and since others have spent many pages and volumes articulating their research, I simply suggest that my understanding of myth is indebted especially to Doniger (1998) from this book and her earlier *Other People's Myths: The Cave of Echoes* (1988); to William Doty's extensive *Mythography* (2000); and to the now-classical works of Emile Durkheim (*The Elementary Forms of the Religious Life*, 1965) and Mircea Eliade (*The Sacred and the Profane*, 1959).
3   *Mise-en-scène* began as a theatrical term but was quickly adapted to early cinema. Literally meaning, 'to put onto stage', *mise-en-scène* has been a serious topic for scholars and critics of film almost since the beginnings of film theory. Good introductions include the chapter 'The Shot: Mise-en-scene', in Bordwell & Thompson (2001: 156–90); and the short book by John Gibbs, *Mise-en-scène: Film Style and Interpretation* (2002).
4   See George Lucas's interview by Bill Moyers (1999); for Andy and Larry Wachowski, see Richard Corliss (1999). A number of religious studies

scholars have written on each of the films. I would highlight, especially, Gordon (1995); Flannery-Dailey & Wagner (2001); and Lyden (2000).

5   In *Alien Sex*, Gerard Loughlin notices close parallels between the cinema, the church and Plato's cave, suggesting, 'the suspension of the real is necessary for faithful living, for being able to see and live by the light that burns in the dark' (2004: 35).

6   Baudrillard argued against the use of his book in *The Matrix*, saying the filmmakers got it wrong. This would be a much deeper philosophical argument than is possible in the space here; see a translated interview with Baudrillard on the topic at: http://www.empyree.org/divers/Matrix-Baudrillard_english.html (accessed 12 July 2007).

7   There are many scholarly books on the subject of Gibson's film. I recommend three of them for their broad take on it: Landres & Berenbaum (2004); Plate (2004b); and Beal & Linafelt (2006).

8   The aspects of bodily sense reception in relation to religion are argued further in my books *Religion, Art, and Visual Culture* (2002) and *Walter Benjamin, Religion, and Aesthetics: Rethinking Religion through the Arts* (2005).

chapter two

1   While I quote directly from Alexander, my understanding of ritual is influenced by Jonathan Z. Smith's *To Take Place* (1987); Victor Turner's *The Ritual Process* (1991); Richard Schechner's *The Future of Ritual* (1993); and Ron Grimes' work in *Deeply Into the Bone* (2000) and *Rite Out of Place* (2006). This is an admittedly limited list, and there is a much lengthier bibliography to which I could refer (including more Grimes, Smith, Turner and Catherine Bell), but what I suggest above lends itself effectively to the study of film.

2   See the previous note for definitions relating to the other aspects.

3   Ronald Grimes' work has been important in maintaining distinctions between 'ritual' and 'media'. They have many things in common, as is argued throughout this book, but cannot simply be equated; see especially the chapter 'Ritual and the Media' (Grimes 2006: 3–13).

4   David Bordwell and Kristin Thompson note this in *Film Art*. Many films, especially action films, have double that number, making for a large job for the editor.

5   From a behind-the-scenes featurette on the DVD, released by MPI Home
    Video in 1991.

chapter three

1   Rachel O. Moore argues that this retelling of 'naïve spectatorship' reas-
    sures 'us of our superior position as spectators, while at the same time
    they enact our felt affinity to the primitive faced with our disappearing
    world' (1999: 4). In noting this, I am deeply grateful for Moore's work
    in her book, and have gleaned a great deal from it. For a contrasting
    position, compare early filmmaker George Méliès' response to that first
    night: 'We were open-mouthed, dumbfounded, astonished beyond
    words in the face of this spectacle' (quoted in Toulet 1995: 15).
2   There have been a number of recent works in film theory relating the
    body to the cinematic experience. Covering similar ground are works
    such as: Steven Shaviro's *The Cinematic Body* (1993); Laura Marks'
    The Skin of the Film (2000); and Vivian Sobchack's *Carnal Thoughts*
    (2004). Each of these works are, in turn, especially indebted to the
    corporeal philosophies of Gilles Deleuze and Maurice Merleau-Ponty.
3   I deal with 'creation as separation' more fully in the introduction to
    *Walter Benjamin, Religion, and Aesthetics: Rethinking Religion through
    the Arts* (2005).
4   Luce Irigaray's feminist critique of Merleau-Ponty is important: that
    Merleau-Ponty gives too much attention to vision (see Irigaray 1993).
    There is much that is culturally gendered and sexed within the aes-
    thetic make up of the body: the 'distant senses' such as the eyes and
    ears are traditionally asserted to be a masculine register, while the
    'proximate senses' such as touch and taste are claimed to be femi-
    nine. Nonetheless, what Merleau-Ponty ultimately does is to show the
    relations, the synaesthesia even, between vision and touch, and I
    think therefore offers many opportunities for rethinking the gender of
    aesthetic construction. Irigaray somewhat acknowledges this, but at
    times seems to reaffirm too much of the 'traditional' sensual rendering
    whereby touch is feminine and vision is masculine.
5   For one interesting take on the prominence of certain faces, see Roland
    Barthes' 'The Face of Garbo' (1972: 56–7).
6   See my articles, 'The Re-creation of the World: Filming Faith' (2003);

and 'Hospitable Vision: Some Notes on the Ethics of Seeing Film' (co-written with Margaret R. Miles; 2004b).

7   See Maya Deren's 'Cinematography: The Creative Uses of Reality' (1987). Also critical to my thinking here is Kaja Silverman's *Threshold of the Visible World* (1996) in which she contrasts an 'idiopathic' identification (seeing sameness, as with most films in the Hollywood system) with a 'heteropathic' identification with the other seen on film. In this way, she articulates a psychoanalytic 'ethics in the field of vision'.

8   I mean 'supplement' in the full etymological sense Jacques Derrida has given to it, as an 'addition' and a 'substitution': 'the supplement adds itself, it is a surplus, a plenitude enriching another plenitude, the fullest measure of presence' (1976: 144), but also, 'if it fills, it is as if one fills a void. If it represents and makes an image, it is by the anterior default of a presence' (1976: 145). This seems a concise way to think about the relation of contemporary cinematics to traditional ritual.

9   No reference is given for the inner J. S. Mill quote.

chapter four

1   The *Rocky* films have been so engrained into the consciousness of millions of people around the world that the massive art museum, opened in 1877, is almost overshadowed in popularity by these footprints, based on the 1976 film. Virtualtourist.com has a page devoted to the Philadelphia Museum of Art, with several dozen reviews of the museum and accompanying images. About one quarter of all the reviews are actually about the 'Rocky' footprints. One entry even blatantly suggests, 'A group of us visited this museum, from "Rocky" fame, on a whim...' as if no one ever went to museums except for their famed background appearance in movies; see: http://www.virtualtourist.com/travel/North_America/United_States_of_America/Pennsylvania/Philadelphia-860659/Things_To_Do-Philadelphia-Philadelphia_Museum_of_Art-R-1.html (accessed 5 June 2005). Also, Tourquest.com offers student travel to popular US destinations, including Philadelphia. From their homepage one reads that you can go to Philadelphia to 'see the historic part of Colonial USA, in its earliest stages!' The first bullet point listed under that 'colonial' city is the fact that you can 'Stand in "Rocky's" footprints atop the steps of the Art

Museum', while four points down is the vague, 'Learn why Philadelphia is considered one of the major building blocks of the U.S.'; see http://www.tourquest.com/ (accessed 5 June 2005).

2   For the best collection on the films from a religious studies standpoint see Kapell & Doty (2004).

3   Thanks are due to my student, Katherine Rodriguez, who discussed her brother's wedding. Also, some of the research in this section was aided by my student assistant Megan Ammann, and I wish to thank her for her help.

4   See http://www.take2weddings.com (accessed 15 March 2008).

5   See http://www.advol.com/wedshops/ceremony.htm (accessed 3 February 2005).

6   See http://www.lovetripper.com/channels/romantic-movie-quotes.html (accessed 3 February 2005).

7   See http://www.partypop.com/themes/BARM0004.html (accessed 25 May 2005). This account is probably a fabricated story, made up to appeal to young people shopping for b'nai mitzvah themes. Nonetheless, the numerous websites displaying ways to do various film themes are very real.

8   What is interesting in the liberal-conservative divide, as an independent study with my student Tiffany Austin revealed this year, is that there is a correspondence between the length of film clips shown (and related biblical passages referred to) and the theo-political divide. In a survey of curriculum resources for various Christian groups, it is clear that the more conservative the church and their corresponding curricula, the shorter the film clips and biblical passages. Conservative churches place more emphasis on shorter biblical passages (usually one to two verses) and shorter film clips (usually one to two minutes), while the mainline churches offer advice for lengthier quotes and clips (often up to ten minutes). However, the theologically conservative churches unabashedly offer the film clips in the main Sunday service while the more liberal churches relegate such cultural interactivity to Adult Education course. Compare conservative publications such as Bryan Belknap's *Group's BlockBuster Movie Illustrations* (2001) and the slightly more left-leaning *Videos that Teach* by Doug Fields and Eddie James (1999) with Abingdon Press's periodical *Reel to Real: Making the Most of the Movies with Youth* (Issue 1.1, 1997).

9   In the tradition of the wedding photographer, many companies have emerged to 'memorialise' – that is, 'take images of' – for example, baptisms, bar mitzvahs and particularly funerals. A company specialising in 'memorial videos' offers the ability to 'Honour a loved one with a beautiful tribute video. This video can also help promote healing for those that are suffering from loss. Instead of focusing on the death, you and your family will be able to focus on the life of … your loved one'; see http://www.essenceoflifevideo.com/memorial/index.html (accessed 6 June 2005). Many other companies offer similar services.

10 See http://www.mitzvahchic.com/index.php (accessed 25 May 2005); see also Oppenheimer (2005).

11 For a brief news story, see: http://www.ananova.com/news/story/sm_1086432.htmlm (accessed 2 June 2005). The website address of the Romanian fan club is http://www.jedi.ro/index.htm (in Romanian).

12 Liz Locke (1999) relates Victor Turner's ideas of *communitas* to the cult following of *The Rocky Horror Picture Show*. She concludes, 'What Turner calls "normative communitas" doesn't only occur at the end of RHPS … It also happens in RHPS communities. The cast members see themselves as more devoted than regular audience members. Their community is held together by fellow thespian aspiration as well as by love of the film'; see also the online site: http://www.rockyhorror.com for further information and statistics.

13 Other cult films include such diverse offerings as *The Wizard of Oz* (1939), *Harold and Maude* (1971), *The Texas Chainsaw Massacre* (1974) and *Eraserhead* (1977).

14 An account of the earliest audience participation rituals at screenings of *The Rocky Horror Picture Show* are given online at: http://www.rockyhorror.com/partbegn.html (accessed 5 June 2005).

15 I have attempted to articulate this 'other-worldliness' further in my article 'The Re-creation of the World: Filming Faith' (2003).

16 Thanks to my colleague Ronald Flowers for insight into the case; see Flowers (2000); and Boston (2005).

17 See the FOE website, which includes a short article by DeMille on 'Why We Need the Ten Commandments': http://www.foe.com/events/ten-commandments.aspx (accessed 15 March 2008).

FILMOGRAPHY

Act of Seeing With One's Own Eyes, The (Stan Brakhage, 1971, US)
Antonia (Antonia's Line) (Marleen Gorris, 1995, Netherlands/Belgium/UK)
L'Arrivée d'un train à la Ciotat (The Arrival of a Train at la Ciotat) (Auguste and Louis Lumière, 1895, France)
Baraka (Ron Fricke, 1992, US)
Big Fish (Tim Burton, 2003, US)
Blue Velvet (David Lynch, 1986, US)
Chelovek s kino-apparatom (Man with a Movie Camera) (Dziga Vertov, 1929, Soviet Union)
Chocolat (Lasse Hallström, 2000, UK/US)
Deconstructing Harry (Woody Allen, 1997, US)
Matrix, The (Andy and Larry Wachowski, 1999, Australia/US)
Nuovo cinema Paradiso (Cinema Paradiso) (Giuseppe Tornatore, 1988, Italy/France)
Passion of the Christ, The (Mel Gibson, 2004, US)
Purple Rose of Cairo, The (Woody Allen, 1985, US)
Rocky (John G. Avildsen, 1976, US)
Rocky Horror Picture Show, The (Jim Sharman, 1975, UK/USA)
Sirius Remembered (Stan Brakhage, 1959, US)
Star Wars (George Lucas, 1977, US)
Tideland (Terry Gilliam, 2005, Canada/UK)
Titanic (James Cameron, 1997, US)
Wavelength (Michael Snow, 1967, Canada/US)

BIBLIOGRAPHY

The most extensive bibliography on religion and film to date is found in Jolyon Mitchell and S. Brent Plate (eds) *The Religion and Film Reader*, 445–57. For the reader interested in a much more comprehensive overview, that is the place to look. Along with the works cited through this book, what I list in the following, somewhat idiosyncratic collection, are those books most important to my argument, the books that have most shaped my thoughts about the religion and film relation. Some of these are strictly film studies works, some are strictly religious studies, while others work in the interdisciplinary regions. Even if the following is a collection of odd bedfellows, all the entries come highly recommended.

Alexander, Bobby C. (1997) 'Ritual and Current Studies of Ritual: Overview', in Stephen D. Glazier (ed.) *Anthropology of Religion: A Handbook*. Westport, CT: Greenwood Press, 139–60.

Allen, Richard (1997) *Projecting Illusion: Film Spectatorship and the Impression of Reality*. Cambridge: Cambridge University Press.

Anon. (1998) 'Girl Gets Titanic Bat Mitzvah', *Associated Press*, 29 October. Available at: http://www.vho.org/News/GB/SRN29-30_98.html#3 (accessed 7 June 2005).

Ariès, Philippe (1974) *Western Attitudes Toward Death*, trans. Patricia M. Ranum. Baltimore: Johns Hopkins University Press, 105–6.

____ (1987) *The Hour of Our Death*. London: Penguin.

Bandy, Mary Lea and Antonio Monda (eds) (2003) *The Hidden God: Film and Faith*. New York: The Museum of Modern Art.

Barthes, Roland (1972) *Mythologies*. New York: Hill and Wang.

Baudrillard, Jean (1988) 'Simulacra and Simulations', trans. Paul Foss, Paul Patton and Philip Beitchman, in Mark Poster (ed.) *Jean Baudrillard: Selected Writings*. Stanford: Stanford University Press, 166–84.

—— (1994) 'On Nihilism', in *Simulacra and Simulations*, trans. Sheila Glaser. Ann Arbor, MI: University of Michigan Press, 159–64.

Bazin, André (1997 [1951]) 'Cinema and Theology', in Bert Cardullo (ed.) *Bazin at Work: Major Essays & Reviews from the Forties & Fifties*, trans. Bert Cardullo and Alain Piette. New York: Routledge, 61–72.

Beal, Timothy K. and Tod Linafelt (eds) (2006) *Mel Gibson's Bible*. Chicago: University of Chicago Press.

Belknap, Bryan (2001) *Group's BlockBuster Movie Illustrations*. Loveland, CO: Group.

Benjamin, Walter (2002 [1936]) 'The Work of Art in the Age of Its Technological Reproducibility', trans. Edmund Jephcott and Harry Zohn, in *Selected Writings: Volume 3, 1935–1938*. Cambridge, MA: Harvard University Press, 101–33.

Berger, Peter (1967) *The Sacred Canopy: Elements of a Sociological Theory of Religion*. New York: Anchor Books.

Bordwell, David and Kristin Thompson (2001) *Film Art: An Introduction*, sixth edition. New York: McGraw Hill.

Boston, Rob (2005) 'Nine Justices, Ten Commandments, Two Important Cases', *Church & State*, 58, 4, April, 4–7.

Bowie, Fiona (2006) *The Anthropology of Religion*, second edition. Malden, MA: Blackwell.

Brakhage, Stan (1978 [1963]) 'Metaphors on Vision', in P. Adams Sitney (ed.) *The Avant-Garde Film*. New York: Anthology Film Archives, 120–8.

Buckland, Warren (2000) *The Cognitive Semiotics of Film*. Cambridge: Cambridge University Press.

Campbell, Joseph and Bill Moyers (1991) *The Power of Myth*. New York: Anchor Books.

Cavell, Stanley (1979) *The World Viewed*. Cambridge, MA: Harvard University Press.

Charney, Leo and Vanessa R. Schwartz (eds) (1995) *Cinema and the Invention of Modern Life*. Berkeley: University of California Press.

Cixous, Hélène, with Catherine Clément (1986) *The Newly Born Woman*, trans. Betsy Wing. Minneapolis: University of Minnesota Press.

Clark, Lynn Schofield (2003) *From Angels to Aliens: Teenagers, the Media and the Supernatural*. Oxford: Oxford University Press.

Corliss, Richard (1999) 'Popular Metaphysics', *Time*, 153, 15, 19 April, 75–6.

Cosandey, Roland, André Gaudreault and Tom Gunning (eds) (1992) *An Invention of the Devil? Religion and the Early Cinema. Une Invention du Diable? Cinéma des Premiers Temps et Religion*. Sainte Foy: Les Presses de l'Université Laval.

Deacy, Christopher (2005) *Faith in Film: Religious Themes in Contemporary Cinema*. Burlington, VT: Ashgate.

Deren, Maya (1965) 'Ritual in Transfigured Time', *Film Culture*, 39, 5–6.

_____ (1987 [1960]) 'Cinematography: The Creative Use of Reality', in P. Adams Sitney (ed.) *The Avant-Garde Film*. New York: Anthology Film Archives, 60–73.

Derrida, Jacques (1976) *Of Grammatology*, trans. Gayatri Chakravorty Spivak. Baltimore: Johns Hopkins University Press.

Deutsch, Eliot (1991) 'Community as Ritual Participation', in Leroy S. Rouner (ed.) *On Community*. Notre Dame, IN: University of Notre Dame Press, 15–26.

Doniger, Wendy (ed.) (1975) *Hindu Myths*. Harmondsworth: Penguin.

—— (1988) *Other People's Myths: The Cave of Echoes*. Chicago: University of Chicago Press.

—— (1998) *The Implied Spider: Politics and Ideology in Myth*. New York: Columbia University Press.

Doty, William G. (2000) *Mythography*, second edition. Tuscaloosa, AL: University of Alabama Press.

—— (2006) 'Myths and Tales in *Big Fish*', *Mythic Passages: The Magazine of Imagination*. Available at: http://www.mythicjourneys.org/newsletter_dec06_doty.html (accessed 15 March 2008).

Douglas, Mary (1992) *Purity and Danger*. London: Routledge.

Drazin, Charles (1999) *Charles Drazin on Blue Velvet*. London: Bloomsbury.

Durkheim, Emile (1965) *The Elementary Forms of the Religious Life*. New York: Free Press.

Dwyer, Rachel (2006) *Filming the Gods: Religion and Indian Cinema*. Abingdon: Routledge.

Eisenstein, Sergei (1992a [1929]) 'The Cinematographic Principle and the Ideogram', in Gerald Mast, Marshall Cohen and Leo Braudy (eds) *Film*

Theory and Criticism: Introductory Readings, fourth edition. New York: Oxford University Press, 127–38.

____ (1992b [1929]) 'A Dialectic Approach to Film Form', in Gerald Mast, Marshall Cohen and Leo Braudy (eds) *Film Theory and Criticism: Introductory Readings*, fourth edition. New York: Oxford University Press, 138–54.

Eliade, Mircea (1987) *The Sacred and the Profane: The Nature of Religion*. San Diego: Harcourt Brace.

Elsaesser, Thomas (ed.) (1990) *Early Cinema: Space, Time, Frame*. London: British Film Institute.

Epstein, Jean (2007 [1924]) 'On Certain Characteristics of *Photogénie*', trans. Tom Milne in Jolyon Mitchell and S. Brent Plate (eds) *The Religion and Film Reader*. London: Routledge, 49–53.

Fabe, Marilyn (2004) *Closely Watched Films: An Introduction to the Art of Narrative Film Technique*. Berkeley: University of California Press.

Ferlita, Ernest and John R. May (1976) *Film Odyssey: The Art of Film as a Search for Meaning*. New York: Paulist.

Fields, Doug and Eddie James (1999) *Videos that Teach*. Grand Rapids, MI: Zondervan.

Flannery-Dailey, Frances and Rachel Wagner (2001) 'Wake Up! Gnosticism and Buddhism in *The Matrix*', *The Journal of Religion and Film*, 5, 2, October. Available at: http://www.unomaha.edu/jrf/gnostic.htm (accessed 15 March 2008).

Flowers, Ronald (2000) 'Breaktime', *Liberty*, 95, 4, July/August, 3–7.

Ford, James (2000) 'Buddhism, Christianity, and *The Matrix*', *The Journal of Religion and Film*, 4, 2, October. Available at: http://www.unomaha. edu/jrf/thematrix.htm (accessed 15 March 2008).

Geertz, Clifford (1973) 'Religion as a Cultural System', in *The Interpretation of Cultures: Selected Essays*. New York: Basic Books, 87–125.

Gibbs, John (2002) *Mise-en-scène: Film Style and Interpretation*. London: Wallflower Press.

Goethals, Gregor (1981) *The TV Ritual: Worship at the Video Altar*. Boston: Beacon Press.

Goodman, Nelson (1978) *Ways of Worldmaking*. Indianapolis: Hackett Publishing.

Gordon, Andrew (1995) '*Star Wars*: A Myth for Our Time', in Joel W. Martin and Conrad Ostwalt (eds) *Screening the Sacred*. Boulder, CO: Westview Press, 73–82.

Greenberg, Gail (2004) http://www.mitzvahchic.com/index.php (accessed 25 May 2005).

Grimes, Ronald (2000) *Deeply Into the Bone: Re-Inventing Rites of Passage*. Berkeley: University of California Press.

_____ (2006) *Rite Out of Place*. Oxford: Oxford University Press.

Heschel, Abraham (1951) *The Sabbath: Its Meaning for Modern Man*. New York: Farrar, Straus, Giroux.

Hirsch, Paul (1992) 'Percussive Editing', in Gabriella Oldham (ed.) *First Cut: Conversations with Film Editors*. Berkeley: University of California Press, 188–9.

Hoover, Stewart M. (2006) *Religion in the Media Age*. London: Routledge.

Ingold, Tim (ed.) (1994) *Companion Encyclopedia of Anthropology*. London: Routledge.

Irigaray, Luce (1993) 'The Invisible of the Flesh', in *An Ethics of Sexual Difference*, trans. Carolyn Burke and Gillian C. Gill. London: Athlone Press, 151–84.

Johnston, Robert K. (2000) *Reel Spirituality: Theology and Film in Dialogue*. Grand Rapids, MI: Baker.

—— (ed.) (2007) *Reframing Theology and Film*. Grand Rapids, MI: Baker.

Kapell, Matthew and William G. Doty (eds) (2004) *Jacking in to the Matrix Franchise: Cultural Reception and Interpretation*. New York: Continuum.

Kickasola, Joe (2004) *The Films of Krzysztof Kieślowski: The Liminal Image*. New York: Continuum.

_____ (2006) 'Contemporary Media and the Evolving Notion of Immediacy', *Quarterly Review of Film and Video*, 23, 299–310.

Kinkade, Patrick T. and Michael A. Katovich (1992) 'Toward a Sociology of Cult Films: Reading *Rocky Horror*', *The Sociological Quarterly*, 33, 2, 191–209.

Kolker, Robert (2002) *Film, Form, and Culture*, second edition. New York: McGraw Hill.

Kracauer, Siegfried (1997) *Theory of Film: The Redemption of Physical Reality*. Princeton: Princeton University Press.

Lacan, Jacques (1978) *The Four Fundamental Concepts of Psychoanalysis*, trans. Alan Sheridan. New York: Norton.

Landres, J. Shawn and Michael Berenbaum (eds) (2004) *After the Passion is Gone*. Walnut Creek, CA: AltaMira Press.

Laquer, Thomas (1992) 'Clio Looks at Corporal Politics', in *Corporal Politics*, eds Donald Hall, Thomas Laquer and Helaine Posner. Cambridge: MIT List Visual Arts Center and Beacon Press, 14–21.

Levinas, Emmanuel (1969) *Totality and Infinity*, trans. Alphonso Lingis. Pittsburgh, PA: Duquesne University Press.

Lindvall, Terry (2001) *The Silents of God: Selected Issues and Documents in Silent American Film and Religion 1903–1925*. Lanham, MD: Scarecrow Press.

Locke, Liz (1999) 'Don't Dream It, Be It': *The Rocky Horror Picture Show* as Cultural Performance', *New Directions in Folklore*, 3. Available at: http://www.temple.edu/isllc/newfolk/rhps1.html (accessed 6 June 2005).

Loughlin, Gerald (2004) *Alien Sex: The Body and Desire in Cinema and Theology*. Oxford: Blackwell.

Lowry, Edward (1985) *The Filmology Movement and Film Study in France*. Ann Arbor, MI: UMI Research Press.

Lyden, John (2000) 'The Apocalyptic Cosmology of *Star Wars*', *Journal of Religion and Film*, 4, 1, April. Available at: http://www.unomaha.edu/jrf/LydenStWars.htm (accessed 15 March 2008).

—— (2003) *Film as Religion: Myths, Morals, and Rituals*. New York and London: New York University Press.

MacDonald, Scott (1993) *Avant-Garde Film*. Cambridge: Cambridge University Press.

—— (2006) *A Critical Cinema 5: Interviews with Independent Filmmakers*. Berkeley: University of California Press.

MacDougall, David (2005) *The Corporeal Image*. Princeton: Princeton University Press.

—— (2006) *The Corporeal Image: Film, Ethnography, and the Senses*. Princeton: Princeton University Press.

McGrath, Charles (2005) 'Terry Gilliam's Feel-Good Endings', *New York Times*, 14 August. Available at: http://www.nytimes.com/2005/08/14/movies/14mcgr.html?ex=1124769600&en=b8eac6b20a90d575&ei=5070&emc=eta1 (accessed 15 August 2005).

McLuhan, Marshall (1964) *Understanding Media: The Extensions of Man*. New York: McGraw Hill.

Marks, Laura (2000) *The Skin of the Film: Intercultural Cinema, Embodiment, and the Senses*. Durham, NC: Duke University Press.

Marsh, Clive (2004) *Cinema and Sentiment: Film's Challenge to Theology*. Milton Keynes and Wanyesboro, GA: Paternoster.

Marsh, Clive and Gaye W. Ortiz (eds) (1997) *Explorations in Theology and Film: Movies and Meaning*. Oxford: Blackwell.

Martin, Joel W. and Conrad E. Ostwalt, Jr (eds) (1995) *Screening the Sacred: Religion, Myth, and Ideology in Popular Film*. Boulder, San Francisco and Oxford: Westview Press.

Mast, Gerald, Marshall Cohen and Leo Braudy (eds) (1992) *Film Theory and Criticism*, fourth edition. New York: Oxford University Press.

May, John R. and Michael Bird (eds) (1992) *Religion in Film*. Knoxville, TN: University of Tennessee Press.

Merleau-Ponty, Maurice (1967) *The Visible and the Invisible*, trans. Alphonso Lingis. Evanston: Northwestern University Press.

_____ (1993) *The Merleau-Ponty Aesthetics Reader*. Evanston: Northwestern University Press.

Metz, Christian (1977) *The Imaginary Signifier*. Bloomington: University of Indiana Press.

Miles, Margaret R. (1996) *Seeing and Believing: Religion and Values in the Movies*. Boston, MA: Beacon Press.

Milner, Marion (1955) 'Role of Illusion in Symbol Formation', in *New Directions in Psychoanalysis*, ed. Melanie Klein. London: Routledge.

Mitchell, Jolyon and Sophia Marriage (eds) (2003) *Mediating Religion: Conversation in Media, Religion and Culture*. London: T & T Clark.

Mitchell, Jolyon and S. Brent Plate (eds) (2007) *The Religion and Film Reader*. London: Routledge.

Mitchell, W. J. T. (2005) *What Do Pictures Want? The Lives and Loves of Images*. Chicago: University of Chicago Press.

Moore, Rachel O. (1999) *Savage Theory: Cinema as Modern Magic*. Durham, NC: Duke University Press.

Morgan, David (2005) *The Sacred Gaze: Religious Visual Culture in Theory and Practice*. Berkeley: University of California Press.

Moyers, Bill and George Lucas (1999) 'Of Myth and Men', *Time*, 26 April, 90–4.

Myerhoff, Barbara (1977) 'We Don't Wrap Herring in a Printed Page', in Sally F. Moore and Barbara Myerhoff (eds) *Secular Ritual*. Assen: Van Gorcum, 199–225.

Nathanson, Paul (1992) *Over the Rainbow: The Wizard of Oz as Secular Myth of America*. Albany: State University of New York Press.

Nichols, Bill (1991) *Representing Reality*. Bloomington, IN: Indiana University Press.

Northrup, Lesley A. (1997) *Ritualizing Women*. Cleveland: Pilgrim Press.

Oppenheimer, Mark (2005) *Thirteen and a Day: The Bar and Bat Mitzvah Across America*. New York: Farrar, Straus and Giroux.

Paden, William (1994) *Religious Worlds*, second edition. Boston: Beacon Press.

_____ (2000) 'World', in Willi Braun and Russell T. McCutcheon (eds) *Guide to the Study of Religion*. London: Cassell, 334–49.

Phalke, D. G. (2007 [1917]) 'The Problem of Capital Formation in the Indian Cinema', in Jolyon Mitchell and S. Brent Plate (eds) *The Religion and Film Reader*. New York: Routledge, 25–6.

Plate, S. Brent (2002) *Religion, Art, and Visual Culture*. New York: Palgrave.

—— (2003a) 'The Re-creation of the World: Filming Faith', *Dialog: A Journal of Theology*, 42, 2, 155–60.

—— (2003b) *Representing Religion in World Cinema: Filmmaking, Mythmaking, Culture Making*. New York: Palgrave Macmillan.

—— (2004a) 'Religion and Film', in the *Encyclopedia of Religion*, second edition. New York: Macmillan Press, 3097–103.

—— (ed.) (2004b) *Re-Viewing the Passion*. New York: Palgrave Macmillan.

—— (2005) *Walter Benjamin, Religion, and Aesthetics: Rethinking Religion through the Arts*. London: Routledge.

Plate, S. Brent with Margaret R. Miles (2004) 'Hospitable Vision: Some Notes on the Ethics of Seeing Film', *Cross Currents*, 54, 1, 22–31.

Runions, Erin (2003) *How Hysterical: Identification and Resistance in the Bible and Film*. New York: Palgrave Macmillan.

Schechner, Richard (1993) *The Future of Ritual*. New York: Routledge.

Schrader, Paul (1972) *Transcendental Style in Film*. New York: Da Capo Press.

Schwartz, David (2005) '*Big Fish*: American museum of the moving image', in *Tim Burton: Interviews*, ed. Kristian Fraga. Jackson, MS: University Press of Mississippi, 176–80.

Shaviro, Steven (1993) *The Cinematic Body*. Minneapolis: University of Minnesota Press.

Silverman, Kaja (1996) *Threshold of the Visible World*. New York: Routledge.

Sison, Antonio (2006) *Screening Schillebeeckx: Theology and Third Cinema in Dialogue*. New York: Palgrave.

Sitney, P. Adams (2002) *Visionary Film: The American Avant-Garde, 1943–2000*, third edition. Oxford: Oxford University Press.

Smith, Jonathan Z. (1982) *Imagining Religion*. Chicago: University of Chicago Press.

—— (1987) *To Take Place: Toward Theory in Ritual*. Chicago: University of Chicago Press.

Sobchack, Vivian (2004) *Carnal Thoughts*. Berkeley: University of California Press.

Souriau, Etienne (1953) *L'Univers filmique*. Paris: Flammarion.

Taggart, Stewart (2001) 'Bad Movie Hurts Jedi Down Under', *Wired News*, 31 August. Available at: http://www.wired.com/news/culture/0,1284,54851,00.html (accessed 6 June 2005).

Taussig, Michael (1999) *Defacement*. Stanford: Stanford University Press.

Tillich, Paul (1964) *Theology of Culture*. New York: Oxford University Press.

Toulet, Emmanuelle (1995) *Birth of the Motion Picture*. New York: Harry Abrams.

Trinh, T. Minh-Ha (1999) *Cinema Interval*. New York: Routledge.

Turner, Victor (1991) *The Ritual Process*. Ithaca, NY: Cornell University Press.

Vaux, Sara Anson (1999) *Finding Meaning at the Movies*. Nashville, TN: Abingdon.

Weisenfeld, Judith (2007) *Hollywood Be Thy Name: African American Religion in American Film, 1929–1949*. Berkeley: University of California Press.

Wright, Melanie J. (2006) *Religion and Film*. London: I. B. Tauris.

INDEX

Covering the full spectrum of contemporary Film Studies, from genres and film movements to critical concepts and technologies, the Short Cuts series is now up to 43-volumes long, with many more on their way. Full details on all titles, including reviews and discounts of up to 20%, can be found at **www.wallflowerpress.co.uk**

CINEMA AND HISTORY
The Telling of Stories
Mike Chopra-Gant

£12.99 / $20.00
978-1-905674-59-6

'This is a very useful book that provides a timely reminder of the complexity of the field of cinema and history ... It asks all the right questions, and stimulates the reader to provide answers by indicating the most fruitful paths to follow.'
– Richard Vela, University of North Carolina

GERMAN EXPRESSIONIST CINEMA
The World of Light and Shadow
Ian Roberts

£12.99 / $20.00
978-1-905674-60-2

'An extremely accessible study of the major works associated with German expressionist cinema. The book provides lucid accounts of several prominent films coupled with illuminating background information about the filmmakers.'
– Brad Prager, University of Missouri

FILM AND PHILOSOPHY
Taking Movies Seriously
Daniel Shaw

£12.99 / $20.00
978-1-905674-70-1

'This lucid and lively book introduces virtually all key topics at the intersection of film and philosophy ... and gives a thorough overview of topics including philosophical film genres, cinematic emotions, movies and morality, and the question of whether films can actually do philosophy.'
– Deborah Knight, Queen's University, Canada

CONTEMPORARY BRITISH CINEMA
From Heritage to Horror
James Leggott

£12.99 / $20.00
978-1-905674-71-8

'This is a comprehensive, detailed survey of British cinema in the Blair era. The scholarship is exemplary, having both range and depth of coverage. Everything is here, from popular genres to art cinema, from independent filmmaking to Lottery-funded cinema.'
– Robert Shail, University of Wales, Lampeter

SHAKESPEARE ON FILM
Such Things as Dreams Are Made Of
Carolyn Jess-Cooke

£12.99 / $20.00
978-1-905674-14-5

'Those who know Shakespeare, films and theory will marvel at this wonderfully intelligent, concise, and helpful book. Those beginning will be drawn in by its clarity and its abundant insights.'
– Richard Vela, University of North Carolina

CRIME FILMS
Investigating the Scene
Kirsten Moana Thompson

£12.99 / $20.00
978-1-905674-13-8

'This compact volume leads us on a whistle-stop tour of our cinematic and televisual fascination with the left-handed form of human endeavour.'
– Mark Bould, University of the West of England

SPECTATORSHIP
The Power of Looking On
Michele Aaron

£12.99 / $20.00
978-1-905674-01-5

'An excellent introduction to one of the most fundamental aspects of film culture. This clear, accessible and witty book summarises existing debates while making its own original and significant contribution in its call for ... an ethics of spectatorship.'
– Paul Sutton, Roehampton University

ROMANTIC COMEDY
Boy Meets Girl Meets Genre
Tamar Jeffers McDonald

£12.99 / $20.00
978-1-905674-02-2

'An indispensible overview ... it unifies previously separate strands of RomCom analysis but also builds upon this synthesis to generate a fresh and compelling account.'
– Diane Negra, University of East Anglia

FILM GENRE
From Iconography to Ideology
Barry Kieth Grant

£12.99 / $20.00
978-1-904764-79-3

'A concise overview of the main theoretical, historical and cultural issues of film genre study ... it will become an essential work on its subject.'
– Stephen Prince, Virginia Tech

ITALIAN NEOREALISM
Rebuilding the Cinematic City
Mark Shiel

£12.99 / $20.00
978-1-904764-48-9

'Everything you could need to know about the cornerstones of the genre, from its sudden birth following Mussolini's time in power, through seven key works, to a brief concluding look at its legacy. An excellent introduction to one of the often mentioned but lesser understood forms of world cinema.'
– *Empire*

DISASTER MOVIES
The Cinema of Catastrophe
(second edition)
Stephen Keane

£12.99 / $20.00
978-1-905674-03-9

'Providing detailed consideration of key movies within their social and cultural context, this concise introduction serves its purpose well and should prove a useful teaching tool.'
– Nick Roddick, *Sight and Sound*

WAR CINEMA
Hollywood on the Front Line

Guy Westwell

£12.99 / $20.00
978-1-9044764-54-0

'War films of each generation reveal the political preoccupations of the eras in which they are made. This compact text succinctly summarises the current scholarship and suggests future projects for interested readers to follow.'
– Peter C. Rollins, *Film & History*

THE NEW HOLLYWOOD
From Bonnie and Clyde
to Star Wars
Peter Kramer

£12.99 / $20.00
978-1-904764-58-8

'Rigorous, thorough and lucid, this book sheds new light on the new Hollywood of the late 1960s and 1970s. By placing the films of the period in a wider historical perspective, it invites us to reconsider this particular era in Hollywood's history and the approach to the study of its films.'
– Steve Neale, University of Exeter

DOCUMENTARY
The Margins of Reality
Paul Ward

£12.99 / $20.00
978-1-904764-59-5

'Provides an interesting history of the genre in conventional terms as well as a fascinating exploration of the ever-widening canon of texts which broadly owe much of their construction to documentary modes.'
– Martin Cairns,
Media Education Journal

NEW DIGITAL CINEMA
Reinventing
the Moving Image
Holly Willis

£12.99 / $20.00
978-1-904764-25-0

'This book delivers a highly readable and much needed survey of the diverse currents coursing through the circuits of digital cinema.'
– Chris Darke, author of
Light Readings: Film Criticism and Screen Arts

MELODRAMA
Genre, Style, Sensibility
John Mercer
and Martin Shingler

£12.99 / $20.00
978-1-904764-02-1

'An excellent introduction to the complex and fluctuating debates about film melodrama … It expands understanding of key concepts related to genre, aesthetics, ideology and problems of reading and response.'
– Christine Gledhill,
Staffordshire University

FILM PERFORMANCE
From Achievement
to Appreciation
Andrew Klevan

£12.99 / \$20.00

978-1-904764-24-3

'It is a pleasure to read and re-read this book about acting in cinema … The book offers itself as an example of a new kind of criticism, deceptively rich and poetically suggestive.'
– Adrian Martin, *Film Studies*

MUSIC IN FILM
Soundtracks and Synergy
Pauline Reay

£12.99 / \$20.00

978-1-903364-65-9

'A thorough overview of the major developments in mainstream film music, this introduction develops into a welcome and much-needed focus on the pop score and soundtrack with excellent and original choices of case study films and performers.'
– David Butler, University of Manchester

FEMINIST FILM STUDIES
Writing the Woman
into Cinema
Janet McCabe

£12.99 / \$20.00

978-1-904764-03-8

'This readable history of the intellectual evolution of feminist film studies emerges after real "road-testing" in the classroom.'
– Diane Negra, University of East Anglia

EARLY CINEMA
From Factory Gate
to Dream Factory
Simon Popple
and Joe Kember

£12.99 / \$20.00

978-1-903364-58-1

'Bringing new perspectives and rigour to the study of film and popular culture, there is a real need for the up-to-date introduction that Popple and Kember provide.'
– Ian Christie, Birkbeck College,

NEW GERMAN CINEMA
Images of a Generation
Julia Knight

£12.99 / \$20.00

978-1-903364-28-4

'Delineates and explains with welcome lucidity how histori-cally specific conditions made possible the birth of the New German Cinema in the 1960s and brought about its demise.'
– Klaus Phillips,
Hollins University

FILM EDITING
The Art of the Expressive
Valerie Orpen

£12.99 / \$20.00

978-1-903364-53-6

'An exceptionally intelligent book about a notoriously elusive subject: editing in various kinds and modes of narrative filmmaking.'
– Brian Henderson, University of Buffalo, SUNY

PRODUCTION DESIGN
Architects of the Screen
Jane Barnwell

'This book is more comprehensive than anything before –
masses of research and opinion
analysed with real insight and
understanding.'
– Stuart Craig,
production designer

£12.99 / $20.00

978-1-903364-55-0

BRITISH SOCIAL REALISM
From Documentary
to Brit Grit
Samantha Lay

'A long-overdue introduction
... it fills an important gap in
the literature and will be of
considerable interest anywhere
that courses on British cinema
are offered.'
– Steve Chibnall, De Montfort
University

£12.99 / $20.00

978-1-903364-41-3

AVANT-GARDE FILM
Forms, Themes
and Passions
Michael O'Pray

'An excellent job of providing
a very readable introduction
... a good starting point for
anyone interested in avant-
garde film.'
– Julia Knight,
University of Luton

£12.99 / $20.00

978-1-903364-56-7

WOMEN'S CINEMA
The Contested Screen
Alison Butler

'An invaluable addition to the
literature, offering new and
valuable material while clarify-
ing vexed, overly-debated
issues once and for all
... Beautifully written.'
– Pamela Church Gibson,
The London Institute

£12.99 / $20.00

978-1-903364-27-7

ANIMATION
Genre and Authorship
Paul Wells

'Absolutely excellent. It clearly
introduces areas which do not
have an adequate literature ...
succinct and precise enough to
be used as a starting point for
students' research.'
– David Huxley, Manchester
Metropolitan University

£12.99 / $20.00

978-1-903364-20-8

MISE-EN-SCÈNE
Film Style
and Interpretation
John Gibbs

'The book is an excellent
introduction not just to *mise-
en-scène* but to the study of
film in general, as well as a
reminder of what serious film
criticism should be about.'
– *Film and Film Culture*

£12.99 / $20.00

978-1-903364-06-2